COLLINS

DIY

PROJECTS IN A

WEEKEND

COLLINS
DIY
PROJECTS IN A
WEEKEND

JACKSON · DAY

HarperCollins*Publishers*

COLLINS
DIY PROJECTS
IN A WEEKEND
CONCEIVED, EDITED AND
DESIGNED AT INKLINK,
GREENWICH, LONDON,
ENGLAND

Text:
Albert Jackson and David Day

Design and art direction:
Simon Jennings

Text editor:
Peter Leek

Illustrators:
Robin Harris and David Day

Studio photography:
Ben Jennings

Editorial photography:
*For a full list of photographers
and copyright owners see
acknowledgments page 128*

First published in 1997
by HarperCollins Publishers,
London

For HarperCollins
Editorial director: Polly Powell

A CIP catalogue record is available
from the British Library

ISBN 0 00 414023 0

Text set in Copperplate and Sabon by
Inklink, London

Printed in Singapore

Jacket design: Simon Jennings
Jacket photograph: Ben Jennings

Some of the text
and illustrations in
Collins
DIY Projects in a Weekend
were previously published in
Collins Complete DIY Manual

CONTENTS

1
A COUPLE OF HOURS

New life
for an old door
10
Clearing a blocked
sink or basin
14
Curing a dripping
overflow
17
Insulating a
hot-water cylinder
19
Lagging your pipes
20
Stopping that
tap dripping
21
Fixing a cold
radiator
23
Making your
front door safe
24
Facelift for an old
fireplace
25

ALLOW A COUPLE OF HOURS

2
A MORNING'S WORK

Putting up curtain
rails
28
Hanging blinds
31
Fitting a better
lock
34
Getting a toilet
cistern
to flush
36
Fitting a new carpet
38
New flooring for
your kitchen or
bathroom
40
Stripping old
wallpaper
44
Reviving your
furniture
46
Looking after
garden furniture
47

ALLOW A WHOLE MORNING

3
A WHOLE DAY

Making windows
burglarproof
50
Papering the ceiling
54
Painting the ceiling
56
Mending creaking
stairs
58
Draughtproofing
your doors
62
Sealing up draughty
windows
66
Putting up new
shelving
68
Patching up
damaged plaster
74
Insulating your loft
78
Quick-and-easy
double glazing
81

ALLOW A WHOLE DAY

4
THE COMPLETE WEEKEND

Laying a small patio
84
Making a real stone
pathway
90
Painting the living
room
92
Refurbishing your
kitchen cabinets
102
Papering the spare
room
104
Blocking out noisy
neighbours
114
Tiling the bathroom
117

ALLOW THE COMPLETE WEEKEND

Glossary of terms
124
Index
125
Acknowledgments
128

INTRODUCTION

Nowadays so many things compete for time and attention that our so-called free time has to be managed as carefully as the working day if we are to fit everything into our busy lives. Doing up our homes often takes second place to more pressing needs, even though there are jobs that have been on our 'must do' lists for months. By giving you attainable targets to aim for and simple instructions to follow, this book will help you break the log jam.

So that you can organize your weekends better, we have selected some of the more essential and popular DIY projects and suggested how much time you need to put aside to complete them. Some are very simple and should take you no longer than an hour or two. Other jobs are more time-consuming, and you may have to put in a whole day or even allow for the entire weekend.

In any case, not everybody works at the same speed. If you are fairly experienced, you will be able to cruise through some of these tasks in less time than we suggest; but if you are tackling a project for the first time, you are bound to be a little hesitant and may find yourself taking longer. And then there are the unforeseen snags that can turn an hour's work into a day of misery! For these reasons, we have suggested sensible cut-off points for those jobs where time matters. If you can see yourself running out of time, try to pace the work so that you can leave a project at a stage where you can conveniently pick it up again the next weekend or over a couple of evenings during the following week.

You can easily waste half a day or more unless you remember to buy all the materials you need in advance. Similarly, check our list of essential tools for each project and make sure you have them to hand and in good working order for the weekend.

Lastly, efficiency depends on doing things in the right order. It is frustrating to come to a job only to find there is a lot of preparatory work you haven't bargained for. We have thought of this too, by including essential preparation as separate pro-jects so that you can include them in your scheme of work.

1

A
COUPLE
OF HOURS

New life
for an old door
10

Clearing a blocked
sink or basin
14

Curing a dripping overflow
17

Insulating a
hot-water cylinder
19

Lagging your pipes
20

Stopping that
tap dripping
21

Fixing a cold radiator
23

Making your
front door safe
24

Facelift for an old fireplace
25

ALLOW A COUPLE OF HOURS

NEW LIFE FOR AN OLD DOOR

The first impression any visitor gets of your home is the front door. If it is smartly painted, with gleaming door pull, knocker and letter plate, the entrance to your house or flat looks attractive and welcoming, but it soon starts to look neglected if you leave the fittings to go dull or rusty and the paintwork becomes chipped or badly weathered. Painting the door with a nice bright colour is easy, but what is the best treatment for the door fittings? Cast-iron door knockers, for example, are usually painted black; but it seems a pity to paint over brass or chrome door furniture, especially as there are clear lacquers to protect them once you've got the metal shining to perfection.

WARNING

Follow manufacturers' safety advice when using paint strippers and wear protective gloves when handling cleaning fluids.

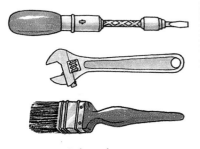

Essential tools

Goggles

Large artist's brush

Paintbrush

Protective gloves

Screwdriver

Spanner

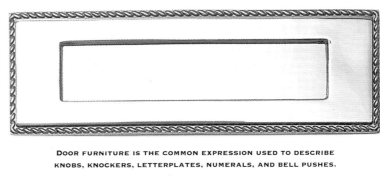

DOOR FURNITURE IS THE COMMON EXPRESSION USED TO DESCRIBE KNOBS, KNOCKERS, LETTERPLATES, NUMERALS, AND BELL PUSHES.

CLEANING BRASS FITTINGS

Brass weathers to a dull brown colour, but it is usually simple enough to buff up dirty fittings with a metal polish. However, if exterior door fittings have been left unprotected, you may have to use a solution of salt and vinegar to soften heavy corrosion before you can start polishing.

Washing with salt and vinegar
Mix one level tablespoonful each of salt and vinegar in 275ml (½ pint) of hot water. Use a ball of very fine wire wool to apply liberal washes of the solution to brass fittings, then wash the metal in hot water containing a little detergent. Rinse and dry the fittings before polishing.

BRASS IS A COMMON MATERIAL USED FOR DOOR FURNITURE AND IF WELL CARED FOR AND POLISHED IT WILL BRIGHTEN ANY ENTRANCE.

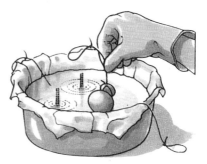

Getting rid of verdigris
Badly weathered brass can develop green deposits called verdigris. This heavy corrosion may leave the metal pitted, so clean it off as soon as possible.

Line a plastic bowl with ordinary aluminium cooking foil. Attach a piece of string to each item of brassware, then place it in the bowl on top of the foil. Dissolve a cup of washing soda in 2.5 litres (4 pints) of hot water and pour it into the bowl to cover the metalware.

Leave the solution to fizz and bubble for a couple of minutes, then lift out the metal fittings with the string. Replace any that are still corroded. If necessary, the process can be repeated using fresh solution and new foil.

Rinse the brass with hot water, dry it with a soft cloth, then polish.

POLISHING YOUR DOOR FITTINGS

Burnish brass door furniture with a 'long-term' brass polish that leaves an invisible chemical barrier on the metal. This inhibits corrosion so that the metal needs cleaning less frequently.

Clean grimy chrome-plated door furniture with lighter fluid, or wash it in warm soapy water containing a few drops of household ammonia. Then burnish the metal with a mild cream chrome polish. Metal polishes should be used sparingly on plated fittings, as consistent polishing will eventually wear through to the base metal.

Lacquering polished brass or chrome
Having polished the metal to a high gloss, use a nailbrush to scrub it with warm water containing some liquid detergent. Rinse the fittings in clean water, then dry them thoroughly with an absorbent cloth.

Paint on acrylic lacquer with a large, soft artist's brush, working swiftly from the top. Let the lacquer flow naturally, and work all round the object to keep the wet edge moving. If you do leave a brush stroke in partially set lacquer, finish the job, then warm the metal (if possible, by standing it on a radiator). As soon as the blemish disappears, remove the object from the heat and allow it to cool gradually in a dust-free atmosphere. If lacquer becomes discoloured or chipped, remove it with acetone, repolish the metal, and then apply fresh lacquer.

TIP ● ● ● ● ● ● ● ● ● ● ● ● ● ● ● ●
Saving time when polishing
Clearly, it would be a chore to remove your door fittings every time you want to polish them, but metal polishes tend to discolour the surrounding paintwork. However, you can protect the paint from abrasive cleaners by using a template cut from thin card which you slip over each fitting. Alternatively, stick low-adhesive masking tape over the paintwork.

You don't have to remove a door fitting, such as a letter plate that has raised edges. The next time you repaint the door, allow the paint to coat the edges, but wipe it from the surface of the fitting with a cloth dampened with white spirit. Once the paint is dry, you can polish the exposed metal without touching the painted woodwork.

CLEANING AND PAINTING CAST-IRON FITTINGS

You can't do a lot with rusty cast-iron door knockers or letter plates until you have soaked them in paraffin for several hours to soften the corrosion. Then you can clean the metal with fine wire wool and paint the bare metal with a rust-inhibiting primer or, alternatively, a proprietary rust-killing jelly or liquid that will remove and neutralize rust.

Some rust killers are self-priming, so no additional primer is required. Otherwise, work a suitable primer into crevices and fixings, and make sure sharp edges and corners are coated generously. Finish the metal with semi-matt black paint.

STRIPPING OLD PAINT FROM DOOR FITTINGS

After years of redecorating, door fittings can become so clogged with paint that it is no longer possible to distinguish their true form and detail. At this stage, it pays to remove the layers of old paint with a proprietary chemical stripper.

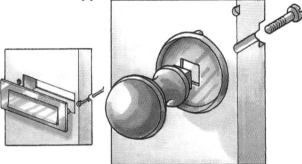

DOOR FITTINGS ARE USUALLY ATTACHED WITH BOLTS

Removing the paint
Even if you intend to strip the paint from the door, it's best to remove the fittings and strip them separately. Arrange them in one or more metal-foil dishes and pour chemical paint stripper into each dish. Stipple the stripper onto the fittings with an old paintbrush to ensure that the chemicals penetrate all the crevices. Leave the stripper to do its work for 10 to 15 minutes, then check that the paint has begun to soften.

Wearing protective gloves and goggles, remove the softened paint from each item with fine wire wool. If there is still paint adhering to a fitting, return it to the dish and apply fresh stripper.

Wash the stripped metal with hot water and dry it thoroughly with thick paper towels. If the fitting is hollow, stand it on a wad of newspaper to allow any water trapped inside to drain away.

ALLOW A COUPLE OF HOURS

Essential tools

Sink plunger

Hydraulic pump

Adjustable wrench

CLEARING A BLOCKED SINK OR BASIN

Don't ignore the early signs of an imminent blockage of the wastepipe from a sink or basin – it only gets worse. If the water drains away slowly, use a proprietary chemical drain cleaner to remove a partial blockage before you are faced with clearing a serious obstruction. Regular cleaning with a similar cleaner also keeps the waste system clear and sweet-smelling. If a wastepipe blocks without warning, try a series of measures to locate and clear the obstruction.

IF THE WATER FROM THE KITCHEN SINK DRAINS AWAY SLOWLY THIS IS USUALLY THE SIGN OF A BLOCKED WASTEPIPE OFTEN CAUSED BY AN ACCUMULATION OF FAT AND FOOD DEBRIS. TRY ONE OF THE REMEDIES OPPOSITE TO RESTORE NORMAL DRAINAGE FUNCTION.

CLEANING THE WASTE-PIPE AND TRAP

In most cases, blockages occur because grease, hair and particles of kitchen debris build up gradually within traps and wastepipes. If water drains away sluggishly, use a cleaner immediately. Follow the manufacturer's instructions carefully, with particular regard to safety. Always wear protective gloves and goggles when handling chemical cleaners, and keep them out of the reach of children.

If unpleasant odours linger after you have cleaned the waste, pour a little disinfectant into the basin overflow.

Using a plunger
If one basin fails to empty while others are functioning normally, the blockage must be somewhere along its individual branch pipe. Before you attempt to locate the blockage, try forcing it out of the pipe with a sink plunger. Smear the rim of the rubber cup with petroleum jelly, then lower it into the blocked basin to cover the waste outlet. Make sure there is enough water in the basin to cover the cup. Block the overflow with a wet cloth, held in one hand, while you pump the handle of the plunger up and down a few times. The waste may not clear immediately if the blockage is merely forced further along the pipe, so repeat the process until the water drains away. If it will not clear after several attempts, try clearing the trap.

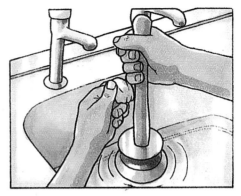

USE A PLUNGER TO FORCE OUT A BLOCKAGE

Now clear the trap
The trap, situated immediately below the waste outlet of a sink or basin, is basically a bent tube designed to hold water that seals out drain odours. Traps become blocked when debris collects at the lowest point of the bend. Place a bucket under the basin to catch the water, then use a wrench to release the cleaning eye at the base of a standard trap. Alternatively, remove the large access cap on a bottle trap by hand. If there is no provision for gaining access to the trap, unscrew the connecting nuts and remove the entire trap.

Let the contents of the trap drain into the bucket, then bend a hook on the end of a length of wire and use it to probe the section of wastepipe beyond the trap. (It is also worth checking outside to see if the other end of the pipe is blocked with leaves.) If you have to remove the trap, take the opportunity to scrub it out with detergent before replacing it.

UNSCREW THE ACCESS CAP ON A BOTTLE TRAP

Another way to clear the branch pipe

Quite often, a vertical pipe from the trap joins a virtually horizontal section of the wastepipe. There should be an access plug built into the joint so that you can clear the horizontal pipe. Have a bowl ready to collect any trapped water, then unscrew the plug by hand. Use a length of hooked wire to probe the branch pipe. If you locate a blockage that seems very firmly lodged, rent a drain auger from a tool-hire company to clear the pipe.

If there is no access plug, remove the trap and probe the pipe with an auger. If the wastepipe is constructed with push-fit joints, you can dismantle it.

TIP ● ● ● ● ● ● ● ● ● ● ● ● ●
The last resort

If a plunger is ineffective in clearing a blocked waste outlet, use a simple hand-operated hydraulic pump. A downward stroke on the tool forces a powerful jet of water along the pipe to disperse the blockage. If it is lodged firmly, an upward stroke may create enough suction to pull it free.

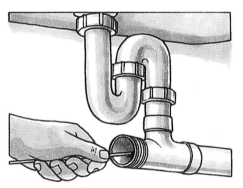

USE HOOKED WIRE TO PROBE A BRANCH PIPE

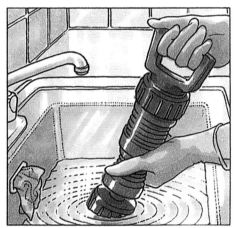

Using a hydraulic pump
Block the sink overflow with a wet cloth. Fill the pump with water from the tap, then hold its nozzle over the outlet, pressing down firmly. Pump up and down until the obstruction is cleared.

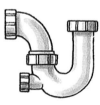

Tubular trap
If the access cap to the cleaning eye is stiff, use a wrench to remove it.

Bottle trap
A bottle trap can be cleared easily, because the whole base of the trap unscrews by hand.

CURING A DRIPPING OVERFLOW

The level of water in a toilet cistern or in the water-storage cistern in the loft is controlled by a hollow float attached to one end of a rigid arm fitted to the water-inlet valve. As the level rises, the water lifts the float until the other end of the arm eventually closes the valve, shutting off the incoming water. If the arm is not adjusted correctly, water continues to flow into the cistern until it escapes to the outside through an overflow pipe. Usually, the solution is to adjust the float arm.

ALLOW A COUPLE OF HOURS

Essential tools
Screwdriver

THE FLOAT ARM WILL ALWAYS BE FOUND IN THE CISTERN BEHIND THE TOILET. IN THIS CASE THE CISTERN IS PANELLED IN BUT IS ACCESSIBLE THROUGH A REMOVABLE SHELF.

ADJUSTING THE FLOAT ARM

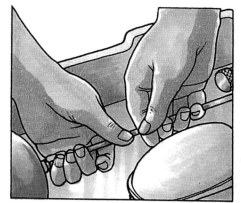

STRAIGHTEN OR BEND A METAL FLOAT ARM

1 *Adjust the float to maintain the optimum level of water, which is about 25mm (1in) below the outlet of the overflow pipe. On some valves the arm is a solid-metal rod. Bend it downward slightly to reduce the water level.*

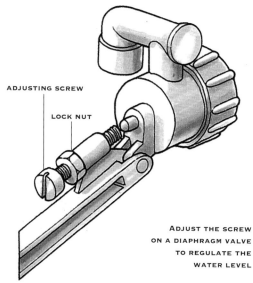

ADJUSTING SCREW

LOCK NUT

ADJUST THE SCREW ON A DIAPHRAGM VALVE TO REGULATE THE WATER LEVEL

2 *The arm on a diaphragm valve has an adjusting screw that presses on the end of a piston. Release the lock nut and turn the screw towards the valve to lower the water level, or away from it to allow the water to rise.*

REPLACING A DAMAGED FLOAT

MODERN PLASTIC FLOATS

Modern plastic floats rarely leak, but old-style metal floats eventually corrode and allow water to seep into the hollow ball. The float gradually sinks until it won't ride high enough to close the valve.

Emergency measures
Unscrew the float and shake it to test whether there is water inside. If you can't replace it for several days, lay the ball on a bench and enlarge the leaking hole with a screwdriver. Pour out the water and replace the float, then cover it with a plastic bag, tying the neck tightly around the float arm.

Thumb-screw adjustment
Some float arms are cranked, and the float is attached with a thumb-screw clamp. To adjust the water level in the cistern, slide the float up or down the rod.

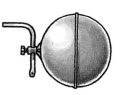

INSULATING A HOT-WATER CYLINDER

ALLOW A COUPLE OF HOURS

Many people think that an unlagged cylinder has the advantage of providing a useful source of heat in an airing cupboard – but in fact it squanders a surprising amount of energy. Even a lagged cylinder should provide ample heat in an enclosed airing cupboard; if not, an uninsulated pipe will do so.

Choosing the jacket
Proprietary water-cylinder jackets are made from segments of mineral-fibre insulation, 80 to 100mm (3¼ to 4in) thick, wrapped in plastic. Measure the approximate height and circumference of the cylinder to choose the right size. If need be, buy a jacket that is too large, rather than one that is too small. Make sure the quality is adequate by checking that it is marked with the British Standard kite mark (BS 5615).

Fitting the jacket
Thread the tapered ends of the jacket segments onto a length of string and tie it round the pipe at the top of the cylinder. Distribute the segments evenly around the cylinder and wrap the straps or tapes provided around it to hold the jacket in place. Spread out the segments to make sure the edges are butted together, and tuck the insulation around the pipes and the cylinder thermostat.

   If you should ever have to replace the cylinder itself, consider substituting a preinsulated version, of which there are various types on the market.

Essential tools
No tools required

TIP ● ● ● ● ● ● ● ● ●
It is also a good idea to insulate hot-water pipes in those parts of the house where their radiant heat is not contributing to the warmth of the rooms (see Lagging your pipes, page 20).

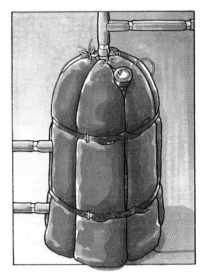

Lagging a hot-water cylinder
Fit a jacket snugly around the cylinder and wrap foamed-plastic tubes around the pipework, especially the vent pipe directly above the cylinder.

Essential tools

Scissors

Craft knife

**Lagging pipes with
foamed-plastic tubes** ☞

*1 Most tubes are pre-
slit along their length
so that they can be
sprung over the pipe . Butt
successive lengths of foam
tube end-to-end, and seal
the joints with PVC
adhesive tape.*

*2 At a bend, cut small
segments out of the
split edge so that the
tube will bend without
crimping. Fit it around the
pipe and seal the closed
joints with tape.*

*3 Where two pipes are
joined with an elbow
fitting, mitre the
ends of the two lengths of
tube, butt them together
and seal with tape.*

*4 Cut lengths of tube
to fit snugly around
a T-joint, linking
them with a wedge-shaped
butt joint, and seal with
tape as before.*

LAGGING YOUR PIPES

When water in a plumbing system is allowed to freeze, it expands and sometimes splits the wall of the pipe or forces a joint apart, with the result that water pours into the house as soon as the ice melts. It therefore pays to insulate cold-water pipes in unheated areas of the building.

CHOOSING INSULATION FOR PIPES

You can wrap pipework in lagging bandages (there are several types, some of which are self-adhesive), but it is generally more convenient to use foamed-plastic tubes designed for the purpose. This is especially true for pipes close to a wall, which may be awkward to wrap.

Foamed-plastic tubes are made in sizes to fit pipes of various diameters: the tube walls vary in thickness from 12 to 20mm (½ to ¾in). More expensive varieties incorporate a metallic-foil backing that reflects some of the heat back into hot-water pipes.

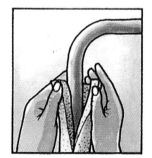

1 SPRING THE TUBE
ONTO A PIPE

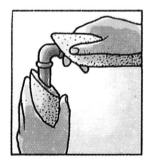

3 CUT MITRES TO ACCOMMODATE
A SOLDERED ELBOW

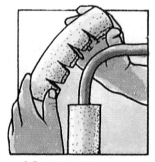

2 CUT THE PLASTIC TUBE
TO FIT A BEND

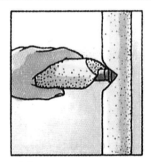

4 CUT A WEDGE-SHAPE BUTT
AT A T-JOINT

STOPPING THAT TAP DRIPPING

There is no need to put up with a dripping tap when it is so easy to replace the washer. Before you dismantle the tap, insert the plug and lay a towel in the bottom of the sink or bath to catch small objects.

Essential tools

Adjustable wrench

Spanner

Screwdriver

TURNING OFF THE WATER

On a modern plumbing system there should be a valve on the supply pipe to the tap which will allow you to turn off the water. On an older system, turn off the main stopcock in order to service the cold-water tap in the kitchen (and other taps under mains pressure). To isolate bathroom taps, cut off the water supply to the storage cistern in the loft by turning off the main stopcock, then open up the taps to drain the cold water.

To work on a hot-water tap, first turn off the boiler or immersion heater and close the valve on the cold-feed pipe to the hot-water cylinder (usually situated in the airing cupboard). Run the hot taps.

Removing a shrouded head from a tap

On most modern taps the head and cover is in one piece. You will have to remove it to expose the headgear nut. Often a retaining screw is hidden beneath the coloured hot/cold disc in the centre of the head. Prise out the disc with the point of a knife. If there's no retaining screw, simply pull the head off.

INSIDE A
TRADITIONAL TAP
1 CAPSTAN HEAD
2 METAL SHROUD
3 GLAND NUT
4 SPINDLE
5 HEADGEAR NUT
6 JUMPER
7 WASHER
8 TAP BODY
9 SEAT
10 TAIL

FITTING A NEW WASHER

If the tap is shrouded with a metal cover, unscrew it by hand or use a wrench, taping the jaws in order to protect the chrome finish.

1 Lift up the cover to reveal the headgear nut just above the body of the tap. Slip a narrow spanner onto the nut and unscrew it until you can lift out the entire headgear assembly.

2 The jumper to which the washer is fixed fits into the bottom of the headgear. In some taps the jumper is removed along with the headgear, but in other types it will be lying inside the tap body.

3 The washer itself may be pressed over a small button in the centre of the jumper; in which case, prise it off with a screwdriver.

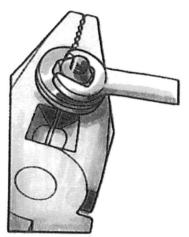

4 If the washer is held in place by a nut, it can be difficult to remove. Allow penetrating oil to soften any corrosion; then, holding the jumper stem with pliers, unscrew the nut with a snug-fitting spanner. (If the nut will not budge, replace both the jumper and the washer.)

Fit a new washer and retaining nut, then reassemble the tap.

FIXING A COLD RADIATOR

If one of your radiators feels cooler at the top than at the bottom, it's likely that a pocket of air has formed in it and is impeding the circulation of the water. Trapped air stops radiators heating up fully, and regular intake of air can cause corrosion. Getting the air out – 'bleeding the radiator' – is a simple matter.

Releasing the air

First switch off the circulation pump – and preferably turn off the boiler too, although that is not vital.

Each radiator has a bleed valve at one of its top corners, identifiable by a square-section shank in the centre of the round blanking plug. You should have been given a key to fit these shanks by the installer; but if not, or if you have inherited an old system, you can buy a key for bleeding radiators at any DIY shop or ironmonger's.

Use the key to turn the shank of the valve anticlockwise about a quarter of a turn. It shouldn't be necessary to turn it further – but have a small container handy to catch spurting water, in case you open the valve too far, plus some rags to mop up water dribbling from the valve. Don't be tempted to speed up the process by opening the valve further than necessary to let the air out – that is likely to produce a deluge of water.

Clearing a blocked valve

If no water or air comes out when you attempt to bleed a radiator, check whether the feed-and-expansion tank in the loft is empty. If the tank is full of water, then the bleed valve is probably blocked with paint.

Close the inlet and outlet valves, at each end of the radiator, then remove the screw from the centre of the bleed valve. Clear the hole with a piece of wire and reopen one of the radiator valves slightly to eject some water from the hole. Close the radiator valve again and refit the screw in the bleed valve. Open both radiator valves and test the bleed valve again.

ALLOW A COUPLE OF HOURS

Essential tools

Radiator key

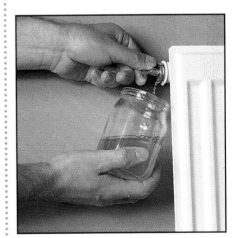

Dispersing the air pocket in a radiator
You will hear a hissing sound as the air escapes. Keep the key on the shank of the valve – then when the hissing stops and the first dribble of water appears, close the valve tightly.

MAKING YOUR FRONT DOOR SAFE

It is not a good idea to open your front door to anyone until you know who is calling. It will take you no more than an hour or two to fix a simple peephole viewer that will enable you to see visitors without opening the door, and a strong security chain which will allow you to check their identification before you admit them.

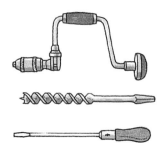

Essential tools

Tape measure

Brace or power drill

Wood bits

Screwdriver

Fitting a viewer

Select a viewer with as wide an angle of vision as possible: you should be able to see someone standing to the side of the door or even crouching below the viewer. Choose one that is adjustable to fit any thickness of door.

Drill a hole the recommended size – usually 12mm (½in) – right through the centre of the door at a comfortable eye level. Insert the barrel of the viewer into the hole from the outside, then screw on the eyepiece from inside.

Attaching a security chain

No special skills are needed to fit a door chain. Fix it securely, just below the lock, by screwing the metal plates to the door and frame.

24

FACELIFT FOR AN OLD FIREPLACE

A traditional fireplace comprises a wooden or painted-metal surround which usually encloses a cast-iron grate. When open fires were the only form of heating, the grate was polished daily with 'black lead', a soft paste made with graphite which nowadays is supplied in toothpaste-like tubes. It produces an attractive silver-black finish that is ideal for highlighting decorative details, but it is not a permanent or durable finish and will have to be renewed periodically. However, since it is easy to apply this is not an arduous chore.

ALLOW A COUPLE OF HOURS

Essential tools

Old toothbrush

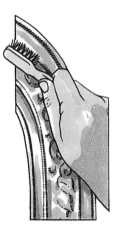

Applying grate polish

Squeeze some polish onto a soft cloth and spread it onto the metal; for best coverage, use an old toothbrush to scrub it into decorative details.

When you have covered the grate, buff the polish to a satin sheen with a clean, dry cloth. Several applications of grate polish makes for a moisture-resistant finish, but it won't prevent rust spots forming if, for example, you accidentally spray the grate when watering pot plants.

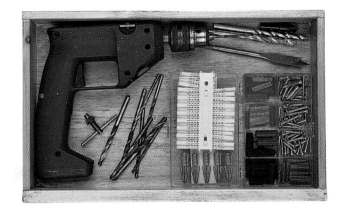

2

A
MORNING'S
WORK

Putting up curtain rails
28
Hanging blinds
31
Fitting a better lock
34
Getting a toilet cistern
to flush
36
Fitting a new carpet
38
New flooring for your
kitchen or bathroom
40
Stripping old wallpaper
44
Reviving your furniture
46
Looking after
garden furniture
47

PUTTING UP CURTAIN RAILS

Window treatments play an important part in the design of any interior and, although the overall size and shape of your windows are fixed, you can emphasize or modify their proportions by careful dressing with curtains. Curtains also provide privacy and help to insulate a room from the sun, cold draughts and noise. Curtains can be bought ready-made in a variety of fabrics and sizes, or you can make your own.

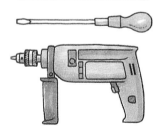

Essential tools

Hammer

Masonry bit

Power drill

Screwdriver

Spirit level

Tape measure

Wood bits

A TRADITIONAL-STYLE BRASS CURTAIN POLE CAN SUPPORT HEAVY DRAPES AND LEND PERIOD CHARM TO AN INTERIOR SCHEME.

SHOULD YOU CHOOSE CURTAIN RAILS OR POLES?

The fabrics you choose for curtaining can make a dramatic difference to an interior, but the method you adopt for hanging curtains can contribute to the decorative style and overall effect, too.

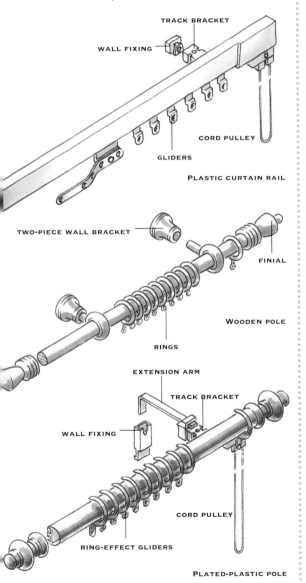

TRACK BRACKET

WALL FIXING

CORD PULLEY

GLIDERS

PLASTIC CURTAIN RAIL

TWO-PIECE WALL BRACKET

FINIAL

WOODEN POLE

RINGS

EXTENSION ARM

TRACK BRACKET

WALL FIXING

CORD PULLEY

RING-EFFECT GLIDERS

PLATED-PLASTIC POLE

Modern curtain rails

Modern rails are made from plastic, aluminium or painted steel. They are available in various styles and lengths and come complete with fixing brackets and glider rings or hooks. Some are supplied ready-corded, which makes drawing curtains easier and protects them from hand soiling.

Although typically used in straight lengths, most rails can be shaped to fit a bay window. Depending on the tightness of the bends, more brackets may be required when fitting a plastic rail into a bay than for metal types. Rails vary in rigidity, which dictates the minimum radius to which they can be bent. Plastic bends more easily when warm.

Traditional-style poles

The curtain poles that were a feature of heavily draped Victorian interiors have become a popular alternative to the low-key track systems of modern times. Made from metal, plastic or wood, they come in a range of plated, painted or polished finishes. Traditional poles are supported on decoratively shaped brackets and are fitted with end-stop finials and large curtain rings. Some designs now conceal corded tracks to provide the convenience of modern curtain rails while retaining old-world charm.

Two wall-mounted decorative brackets are normally used to support curtain poles, but a central bracket may be required to support heavy fabrics or long poles. Plated-plastic tracked versions with ring-effect gliders are available in a range of lengths and are mounted on angle brackets. Light-weight slim poles are also made for sheer curtains or nets. These are fitted with side-fixing or face-fixing sockets.

Screwing a Rail or Pole to the Wall

Draw a guideline at a suitable height above the window opening, then plot the positions for the brackets along the line. Drill holes for wall plugs when you are fixing into masonry walls. The screws must penetrate right into the structural material, not just into the plaster. Screw directly into the wood framing of a partition wall, and use self-tapping screws or cavity fixings for metal lintels.

If it proves difficult to get a secure fixing at all the marked positions, screw a 25mm (1in) thick batten to the wall on which to mount the brackets. You can paint the batten to match the wall or cover it with wallpaper.

In some cases, you can screw light-weight fixing brackets directly to the wooden architrave of a traditional sliding sash or casement window.

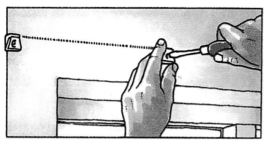

ALIGN THE BRACKETS WITH A LINE MARKED ON THE WALL

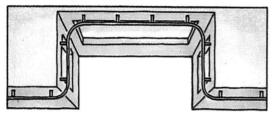

SUPPORTING THE RAIL IN A BAY WINDOW
FIX A RAIL-SUPPORT BRACKET ON EACH SIDE OF A BEND.

Fixing to the Ceiling

In a modern house it may be more convenient to mount curtain track on the ceiling.

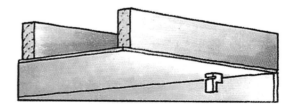

1 Joists that run at right angles to the wall provide a fixing for placing curtain track at any distance from the wall. Drill pilot holes into the joists and screw the brackets in place.

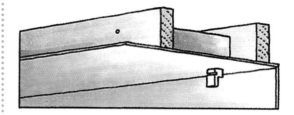

NAIL NOGGINGS BETWEEN JOISTS

2 Joists that run parallel to the wall need noggings nailed between them at the required fixing points. Skew-nail the noggings flush with the ceiling.

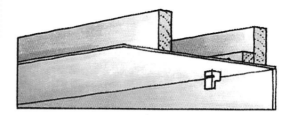

NAIL A BATTEN TO THE JOIST

3 If the required position is close to the original joist, nail a 50 x 50mm (2 x 2in) batten to the face of the joist to provide fixing points for the curtain track.

HANGING BLINDS

ALLOW A WHOLE MORNING

Blinds provide simple, attractive and sometimes sophisticated ways of screening windows. Most are available in standard sizes, but they can be made to measure or cut to size at home. Although simple in appearance, some blinds incorporate refined opening-and-closing mechanisms.

Essential tools

Tape measure

Spirit level

Power drill

Masonry bits

Wood bits

Screwdriver

Hammer

Pliers

Tenon saw

Scissors

YOU CAN BUY ROLLER BLIND MATERIAL TO EITHER DIFFUSE OUTSIDE LIGHT OR TO BLOCK IT COMPLETELY. VENETIAN BLINDS PROVIDED MORE CONTROL OF THE LIGHT LEVEL BUT ARE OFTEN MORE EXPENSIVE.

EASY-TO-FIT ROLLER BLINDS

A wide range of low-cost roller blinds can be bought in kit form. A typical kit consists of a wooden roller with two end caps, one of them spring-loaded to work the blind, two support brackets, a narrow lath, and a pull cord with a knob. Similar kits have aluminium rollers with a different type of return mechanism. Rollers come in several lengths; unless you find one that fits your window exactly, get the next largest size and cut it to the required length. You can buy fabric separately and cut it to width and length.

Fitting a wooden roller

If you decide to fit the roller inside the window recess, place the brackets in the top corners of the window frame. Remove the right-hand end cap by pulling out the round pin from the roller. Cut the roller to fit between the brackets, replace the cap and drive in the pin.

If you want to hang the roller outside the window recess, cut the roller 100mm (4in) longer than the width of the opening. Fit the brackets by drilling and plugging the wall.

Attaching the fabric

Roller-blind fabric must be non-fraying to avoid hems at the sides, and it should be cut precisely or it will not run evenly on the roller. Cut the width to fit between the two end caps, and the length to cover the window plus an extra 200mm (8in).

Make a bottom hem 6mm (¼in) wide, then turn it up to form a sleeve for the lath. Glue and tack the other end of the fabric to the roller, taking care to align the top edge with the roller's axis. Fix the pull cord to the lath with the small screws provided.

Adjusting the roller action

To adjust a spring-loaded action, hold the roller with its flat peg on the left and roll the fabric up so that it hangs from the roller's far side. Place the roller in the brackets and unroll the blind completely; then make it return by giving it a slight pull to release the spring catch. If it returns sluggishly, pull it halfway down, then lift it off the brackets, roll it up fully by hand and replace it. If it now flies back too violently, take the rolled-up blind off the brackets, unwind it a little and replace it.

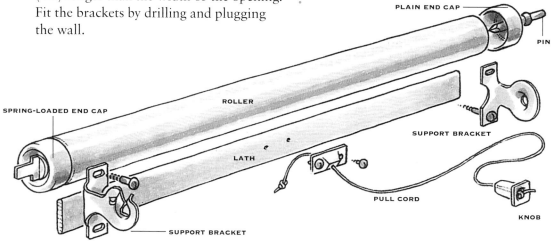

COMPONENTS OF A TYPICAL SPRING-LOADED ROLLER KIT

VENETIAN BLINDS

Horizontal blinds, or Venetian blinds as they are more often called, provide a stylish treatment for most windows. They come in a range of standard sizes, and can be made to measure. They are usually made of metal and are available in a range of coloured finishes, including special effects such as mirror, marble and perforated slats. Wooden-slat versions are also made.

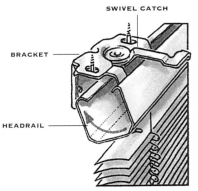

LOCATE THE HEADRAIL ON BRACKETS

Putting up a Venetian blind
If you plan to hang the blind in a window recess, measure the width at the top and bottom of the opening. If the dimensions differ, use the smaller one. Allow about 9mm (⅜in) clearance at each end. Screw the fixing brackets in place so that the blind, when hanging, will clear any window catches or handles. Set the end brackets about 75mm (3in) in from the ends of the blind's headrail.

Mount the headrail in the brackets. Some are simply clamped, while others are locked in place by a swivel catch on each bracket. Raise and lower the blind to check the mechanism is working freely. To lower the blind, pull the cord across the front of the blind, to release the lock mechanism, and let it slide through your hand. Tilt the slats by rotating the control wand.

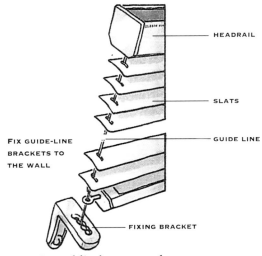

Hanging a blind at an angle
Venetian blinds can be specified for use on a sloping window. Thread the guide lines (they prevent the blind sagging) through holes punched in the slats. These lines are fixed at each end to the headrail and are held taut by fixing brackets at the bottom.

SOPHISTICATED VERTICAL BLINDS
Like Venetian blinds, vertical blinds suit simple modern interiors and work well with large picture windows and patio doors. The blinds hang from an aluminium headtrack that houses the mechanism and is fixed to brackets screwed to the wall or ceiling; the vanes are simply clipped into hooks on the headtrack and linked together by short chains at the bottom. Weights fitted into bottom pockets ensure that the vanes hang straight.

Fixing the track
Mark a guide line on the wall, ceiling or window soffit. Allow sufficient clearance for the rotating vanes to clear obstacles such as window or door handles. Drill, plug and screw the mounting brackets in place and clip the track into the brackets.

Hang the preassembled vanes on the headtrack hooks, first checking that the hooks are facing the same way and that you are attaching the vanes with the seams facing in the same direction.

Essential tools

Brace or power drill

Bradawl

Chisel

Craft knife

G-cramp

Mallet

Marking gauge

Padsaw or jigsaw

Screwdriver

Try square

Wood bits

Night latch
This type of lock alone does not provide adequate security.

Mortise sashlock
Suitable for back and side doors that are used frequently.

FITTING A BETTER LOCK

The door by which you leave the house – usually the front door – needs a particularly strong lock, because it can't be bolted from inside except when you are at home. Don't rely entirely on an old-fashioned night latch, which offers no security at all – it is only as strong as the screws holding it to the door, and a thief can easily break a pane of glass to operate it or simply slide back the bolt with a credit card. Fit a mortise lock, inserted into a slot cut in the edge of the door, where it cannot easily be tampered with. There are various patterns to suit the width of the door stile and the location of the door.

Mortise lock
Use this type of lock on your front door.
1 LOCK BODY
2 FACEPLATE
3 STRIKING PLATE

Selecting the right mortise lock
A mortise sashlock is suitable for back and side doors. It has a handle on each side that operates a springbolt, and a key-operated deadbolt which can't be pushed back once the door is closed. Purely key-operated mortise locks are best for final-exit doors where no handle is necessary. Any exterior-door lock should conform to BS 3621: this is a British Standard which ensures that the lock has a minimum of 1000 key variations, is proof against 'picking' and is strong enough to resist drilling, cutting or forcing. Some locks are intended for right-hand opening doors.

INSERTING THE LOCK

Wedge the door open, so that you can work conveniently on the closing edge.

1 *Scribe a line centrally on the edge of the door with a marking gauge, and use the lock body as a template to mark the top and bottom of the mortise.*

2 *Choose a drill bit that matches the thickness of the lock-body and drill out the majority of the waste wood within marked lines. Square up the edges of the mortise with a chisel until the lock fits snugly in the slot.*

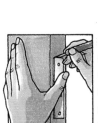

3 *Mark around the edge of the faceplate with a knife, then chop a series of shallow cuts across the waste wood with a chisel. Pare out the recess until the faceplate (including its thin brass coverplate, if fitted) is flush with the edge of the door.*

4 *Hold the lock against the face of the door and mark the centre of the keyhole with a bradawl. Clamp a block of scrap timber to the other side of the door over the keyhole position and drill right through*  *on the centre mark (the block prevents the drill bit splintering the face of the door as it bursts through on the other side). Using a padsaw or power jigsaw, cut out a slot for the keyhole on both sides of the door.*

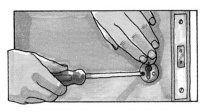

5 *Screw the lock into its recess and check its operation, then attach its coverplate. Finally, screw the escutcheons over the keyholes.*

6 *With the door closed, operate the bolt; it may incorporate a marking device to gauge the position of the striking plate on the doorframe. If it doesn't have a marking device, shoot the bolt fully open, then push the door to and draw round the bolt on the face of the frame.*

7 *Mark out and cut the mortise and recess for the striking plate, as described for the mortise lock itself.*

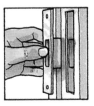

Essential tools
....
Adjustable wrench
....
Pliers
....

Three-part siphon
*This type of siphon can
be dismantled for
replacement of the flap
valve without having to
shut off the water or drain
the cistern.*

Inside your cistern☞
*The components of a
direct-action WC cistern.*
1 OVERFLOW
2 FLOAT
3 FLOAT ARM
4 FLOAT VALVE
5 ONE-PIECE SIPHON
6 WIRE LINK
7 FLUSHING LEVER
8 FLAP VALVE
9 PERFORATED PLATE
10 SEALING WASHER
11 RETAINING NUT
12 FLUSH-PIPE CONNECTOR

GETTING A TOILET CISTERN TO FLUSH

When you depress the flushing lever on your toilet cistern, it lifts a perforated plastic or metal plate at the bottom of an inverted U-bend tube (siphon) that is fixed to the base of the cistern. As the plate rises, the perforations are sealed by a flexible plastic diaphragm (flap valve), so that the plate can displace a body of water over the U-bend to promote a siphoning action. The water pressure behind the diaphragm lifts it again so that the contents of the cistern flow up through the perforations in the plate, over the U-bend and down the flush pipe. As the water level in the cistern drops, so does the float, opening the float valve to refill the cistern.

If the cistern will not flush until the lever is operated several times, the flap valve probably needs replacing. If the flushing lever feels slack, check that the wire link at the end of the flushing arm is intact.

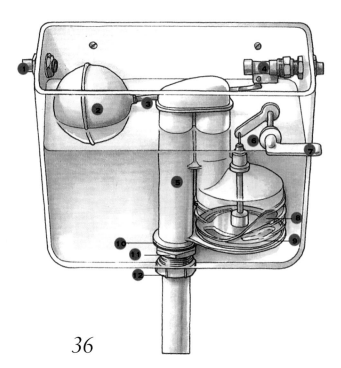

CHANGING THE FLAP VALVE

If the WC cistern will not flush first time, take off the lid and check that the water level is up to the internal mark and that the flushing lever is actually operating the mechanism. If it seems to be working normally, replace the flap valve in the siphon.

1 Before you service a one-piece siphon, shut off the water by tying the float arm to a stout batten placed across the cistern. Flush the cistern.

2 Use a large wrench to unscrew the nut that holds the flush pipe to the underside of the cistern. Move the pipe to one side.

3 Release the remaining nut which clamps the siphon to the base of the cistern. A little water will run out as you loosen the nut, so have a bucket handy. (The siphon may be bolted to the base of the cistern instead of being clamped by a single retaining nut.) Disconnect the flushing arm and ease the siphon out of the cistern.

4 Lift the plastic diaphragm off the metal plate and replace it with one of the same size. Reassemble the entire flushing mechanism in the reverse order and attach the flush pipe to the cistern.

TIP
Making a new wire link
Retrieve the pieces of broken link from the cistern, then bend a new link from a piece of thick wire. If you have thin wire only, twist the ends together with pliers to make a temporary repair.

Essential tools

Bolster

Craft knife

Hammer

Junior hacksaw

Knee kicker

Scissors

Straightedge

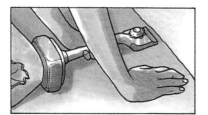

Using a knee kicker
The only special tool required for laying carpet is a knee kicker for stretching it. It has a toothed head, which is pressed into the carpet while you nudge the end with your knee. You can hire a knee kicker from a carpet supplier.

FITTING A NEW CARPET

Some people prefer to loose-lay carpet, relying on the weight of furniture to stop it moving around. However, a properly stretched and fixed carpet looks much better and, provided you are carpeting a fairly simple rectangular room, it isn't difficult to accomplish.

WHY UNDERLAY IS IMPORTANT
A carpet benefits from a resilient cushion laid between it and the floor – it is more comfortable to walk on and the carpet lasts longer. Without an underlay, the divisions between the floorboards will begin to show as dirty marks on a pale carpet as dust from the gaps begins to emerge.

An underlay can be a thick felt or a layer of foamed rubber or plastic. When you buy a foam-backed or rubber-backed carpet, the underlay is an integral part of the floorcovering. In theory, rubber-backed or foam-backed carpets need no additional underlay, but floorboards can still show through cheaper qualities.

In addition, it is worth laying rolls of brown paper or synthetic-fibre sheet over the floor to stop dust and grit working their way into an underlay and to prevent rubber-backed carpet sticking to the floor.

HOW TO FIX YOUR CARPET TO THE FLOOR

LAYING THE CARPET

There are different methods for holding a carpet firmly in place, depending on the type of carpet you are laying.

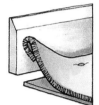

Carpet tacks
Along each edge of the carpet, a 50mm (2in) strip is folded under and nailed to a wooden floor with improved cut tacks about every 200mm (8in). You can usually cover the tack head by rubbing the pile with your fingertips. When using this method, the underlay should be laid 50mm (2in) short of the skirting to allow the carpet to lie flat along the edge.

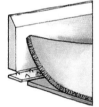

Gripper strips
These wooden or metal strips have fine metal teeth which grip the woven foundation. They are not really suitable for rubber-backed carpets, although they are used. Nail the strips to the floor, 6mm (¼in) from the skirting, with the teeth pointing towards the wall. Cut short strips to fit carpet into doorways and alcoves. Glue gripper strips to a concrete floor. Cut underlay up to the edge of each strip.

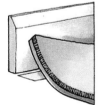

Double-sided tape
Use adhesive tape for rubber-backed carpets only. Stick 50mm (2in) tape around the perimeter of the room; then, when you are ready to fix the carpet, peel off the protective paper layer from the adhesive tape.

If you are laying a separate underlay, join neighbouring sections with short strips of carpet tape or secure them with a few tacks to stop them moving.

Roll out the carpet, butting one machine-cut edge against a wall, and fix that edge to the floor; make sure that any pattern runs parallel to the main axis of the room.

Stretch the carpet to the wall directly opposite and temporarily fix it with tacks, or slip it onto gripper strips. Don't cut the carpet yet. Work from the centre towards each corner, stretching and fixing the carpet, then do the same at the other sides of the room.

Cut a triangular notch at each corner so that the carpet will lie flat. Adjust the carpet until it is stretched evenly, then fix it permanently. When you are using tape or gripper strips, press the carpet into the angle between skirting and floor with a bolster chisel; trim with a knife held at 45 degrees to the skirting. Tuck the cut edge behind the strip with the bolster.

Fitting a threshold bar across the door
Cut the carpet to fit around the doorframe on both sides of the opening, and make a straight cut from one side to the other. Fit a single- or double-sided threshold bar over the cut edge of the carpet.

TOP
DOUBLE THRESHOLD BAR
BOTTOM
SINGLE THRESHOLD BAR

39

Essential tools

Adhesive spreader

Bolster

Craft knife

Home-made scriber

Scissors

Straightedge

Sheet vinyl is available in a wide range of colours and patterns. To ensure it lays as flat as possible, leave the vinyl in the room for 24 to 48 hours before laying it, preferably opened flat or at least stood on end, loosely rolled.

NEW FLOORING FOR YOUR KITCHEN OR BATHROOM

Sheet vinyl is ideal wall-to-wall floorcovering for kitchens, utility rooms and bathrooms, where you are bound to spill water from time to time. It is straightforward to lay if you follow a systematic routine.

Unbacked vinyl

Sheet vinyl is made by sandwiching the printed pattern between a base of PVC and a clear protective PVC covering. All vinyls are relatively hard-wearing, but some have a thicker, reinforced protective layer to increase their durability; ask your supplier which type will suit your needs best. There is a vast range of colours, patterns and textures from which to choose.

Backed vinyl

Backed vinyl has similar properties to the unbacked type, with the addition of a resilient underlay to make it softer and warmer to walk on. The backing is usually a cushion of foamed PVC.

LAYING SHEET VINYL

Before you lay a sheet of vinyl floor-covering, make sure the floor is flat and dry. Vacuum the surface and nail down any loose floorboards. Take out any unevenness by screeding a concrete floor or hardboarding a wooden one. A concrete floor must have a damp-proof membrane; a ground-level wooden floor must be ventilated below. Don't lay vinyl over boards that have recently been treated with wood preserver.

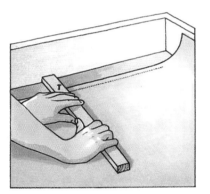

1 Assuming there are no seams, start by fitting the vinyl against the longest wall first. Pull the vinyl away from the wall by approximately 35mm (1½in); make sure it is parallel with the wall or the main axis of the room. Drive a nail through a wooden lath about 50mm (2in) from one end, and use the nailed lath to scribe a line following the skirting. Cut the vinyl with a knife or scissors and slide the sheet up against the wall.

To get the rest of the sheet to lie as flat as possible, cut a triangular notch at each corner. Make a straight cut down to the floor at external corners. Remove as much waste as possible, leaving 50 to 75mm (2 to 3in) turned up all round.

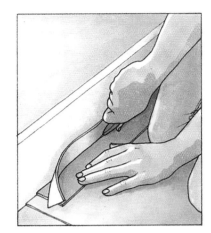

2 Press the vinyl into the angle between skirting and floor with a bolster. Align a metal straightedge with the crease and run along it with a sharp knife held at a slight angle to the skirting. If your trimming is less than perfect, nail a cover strip of quadrant moulding to the skirting.

Fit the vinyl around the doorframe by creasing it against the floor and trimming the waste. Make a straight cut across the opening and fit a threshold bar over the edge of the sheet.

Modern vinyls can be loose-laid but you may prefer to glue the edges, especially along a door opening. Peel back the edge and spread a band of the recommended flooring adhesive with a toothed spreader, or use a 50mm (2in) wide double-sided adhesive tape.

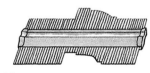

Profile gauge
A profile gauge is a useful tool for copying the shape of door mouldings or pipework; it provides a pattern that helps you fit soft flooring accurately.

Fitting vinyl flooring around doorways
Cut a notch at each of the corners and trim around the doorframe.

Cutting around a toilet or washbasin
To fit around a WC pan or basin pedestal, fold back the sheet and pierce it with a knife just above floor level; draw the blade up towards the edge of the sheet. Make triangular cuts around the base, gradually working around the curve until the vinyl sheet can lie flat on the floor. Crease and cut off the waste.

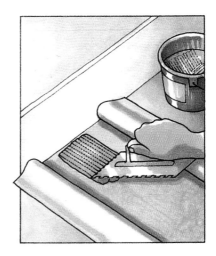

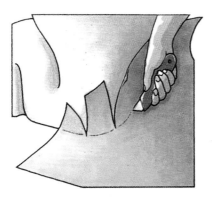

Joining strips of vinyl
If you have to join widths of vinyl, scribe one edge to the wall, then overlap the free edge with the second sheet until the pattern matches exactly. Cut through both pieces with a knife, then remove the waste strips. Without moving the sheets, fold back both cut edges, apply tape or flooring adhesive and press the join together.

SERRATED TROWEL

VINYL FLOORING IS THE IDEAL CHOICE FOR KITCHENS.
SOME MANUFACTURERS, PARTICULARLY OF THE MORE
EXPENSIVE RANGES, RECOMMEND THAT YOU HAVE IT
PROFESSIONALLY FITTED. HOWEVER, IF YOU FOLLOW
THE INSTRUCTIONS SET OUT ON THE PREVIOUS PAGES
SHEET VINYL IS VERY SIMPLE TO CUT AND LAY.

Essential tools

Large paintbrush

Scraper

Paper scorer

Steam stripper

Steam stripper
You can hire a large industrial model or buy a lightweight steam stripper with its own reservoir. Hold the tool's sole plate against the wall until the steam penetrates and softens the wallpaper, then remove it with a scraper. Wash the stripped wall to remove traces of paste.

See also:
Painting the ceiling, page 56
Painting the living room, page 92
Papering the ceiling, page 54
Papering the spare room, page 104
Patching up damaged plaster, page 74

STRIPPING OLD WALLPAPER

Because scraping off old wallcoverings is a necessary preliminary to practically all decorating schemes, it is included here as a project in its own right. Provided the room is not too big and there are no unexpected snags, it should not take you more than half a day to scrape off conventional wallpaper. Stripping specialized wallcoverings or painted wallpaper may take a little longer. Add an appropriate length of time to your decorating schedule.

Eradicating mould growth
Where mould growth is affecting wallpaper, soak it with a warm water-and-bleach solution, then scrape off the paper and burn it. Wash the wall with fresh bleach solution.

Scraping off the paper

To soften the old wallpaper paste, soak the paper with warm water mixed with a little washing-up liquid, or use a proprietary stripping powder or liquid.

Conventional wallpaper
Apply the water with a sponge or house-plant sprayer. Repeat and leave the water to penetrate for 15 to 20 minutes.

Use a wide metal-bladed scraper to lift the softened paper, starting at the seams. Take care not to dig the points of the blade into the plaster. Resoak stubborn areas of paper and leave them for a few minutes before stripping.

Electricity and water are a lethal combination: where possible, dry-strip around switches and sockets. If the paper cannot be stripped dry, switch off the power at the consumer unit when you come to strip around electrical fittings, and unscrew the faceplates so that you can get at the paper trapped behind them. Do not use a sprayer near electrical accessories.

Collect all the stripped paper in plastic sacks, then wash the wall with warm water containing a little detergent.

Scoring a washable wallpaper
Washable wallpaper has an impervious surface film, which you must break through to allow the water to penetrate to the adhesive.

Use a wire brush or a serrated scraper to score the surface, then soak it with warm water and stripper. It may take several applications of the liquid before the paper begins to lift.

Stripping painted wallcoverings
Use a wire brush or home-made scorer to scratch the surface, then soak the paper with warm water plus a little paper stripper. Painted papers (and washables, too) can easily be stripped using a steam stripper (see opposite). Hold the stripper's sole plate against the paper until the steam penetrates, then remove the soaked paper with a wide-bladed scraper.

Peeling vinyl wallcoverings
Vinyl wallcovering consists of a thin layer of vinyl fused with a paper backing. To remove the vinyl, lift both bottom corners of the top layer of the wallcovering, then pull firmly and steadily away from the wall. Either soak and scrape off the backing paper or, if you want to leave it as a lining paper, smooth the seams with medium-grade abrasive paper, using very light pressure to avoid wearing a hole.

Painting over old wallpaper
For best results, it is always best to strip off an old wallcovering before you hang a new one. However, if the existing paper is perfectly sound, you can paint it with emulsion or oil paints (but be warned: it will be more difficult to remove in the future). Strong reds, greens or blues may show through the paint, as will a pattern printed with metallic inks; mask them by applying an aluminium spirit-based sealer. Do not paint vinyl wallcoverings, except for blown vinyl.

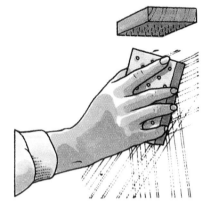

A home-made wallpaper scorer
Drive some nails through a block of softwood measuring about 150 x 125 x 25mm (6 x 5 x 1in), so that the points just protrude.

Essential tools

Paintbrush

Choosing polish

A good polish should be a blend of beeswax and a hard polishing wax such as carnauba. Some contain silicones to make it easier to achieve a high gloss. Polishes range from practically colourless to various shades of brown, which are used to darken the wood.

You can buy flat tins of polish with a thick paste-like consistency. Alternatively, use a liquid wax polish which you can brush onto the wood.

Although it is very attractive, wax polish is not a hard-wearing finish and should be used indoors only.

REVIVING YOUR FURNITURE

It is no secret that a lot of DIY projects represent hard work, but wax polishing furniture is not one of them. It's a rewarding job, and one that is so easy to accomplish that even complete beginners are able to achieve excellent results. A wax polish will preserve and maintain another finish, or can be used as a finish itself.

Polishing new wood

If you want to wax-polish a new piece of furniture or a piece you have stripped back to bare wood, seal it first with one coat of clear varnish (or French polish on fine furniture). This will stop the wax polish being absorbed too deeply into the wood and provides a slightly more durable finish.

Cleaning off old polish

Before waxing old furniture, clean it first to remove deposits of dirt and possibly an old wax dressing. Dip very fine wire wool into white spirit and rub in the direction of the grain. Don't press too hard – as you want only to remove wax and dirt, without damaging the finish below. Wipe the cleaned surface with a cloth dampened with white spirit, and leave to dry before repolishing.

Applying the polish

Apply one coat of paste wax polish with a soft-cloth pad. About 15 minutes later, use a ball of very fine wire wool to apply another coat, rubbing in the direction of the grain. After about four or five coats, leave the wax to harden overnight before burnishing with a duster.

If you prefer to use liquid wax, brush on an initial sealer coat; then an hour later pour more polish onto a cloth pad and rub it in with a circular motion. Follow up by rubbing parallel with the wood grain. Add a third coat if required. Leave the polish to harden overnight, then bring to a high gloss by burnishing vigorously with a soft duster.

LOOKING AFTER GARDEN FURNITURE

Good-quality wooden furniture is made to stand outside for years without any noticeable deterioration. However, it pays to check it over during early spring to make sure it is in good condition, so you can enjoy the garden as soon as the weather warms up.

Make sure the joints are sound and tighten up any bolts or screw fixings. Use fine wire wool or an abrasive nylon pad to remove traces of mould growth or tree resin, and then touch up the finish if it is showing signs of wear or looks dry and dowdy.

If old varnish or paint is starting to flake or split, it may be worth stripping it with a chemical paint remover so you can apply a finishing oil instead (see right). A modern oil finish is ideal for exterior furniture and joinery: it is easy to apply and requires no more than annual maintenance to protect any wood from weathering and to preserve its appearance. Suitable finishes are usually marketed as Danish oil or teak oil.

If your furniture is already oiled, treat all surfaces with one coat of fresh oil and wipe off the excess immediately.

ALLOW A WHOLE MORNING

Essential tools
Paintbrush

Oiling stripped wood
The most efficient way to apply a finishing oil to bare wood is to rub it in with a pad of soft, lint-free rag. Don't store oily rags: keep them in a sealed tin while the job is in progress, then unfold them and leave them outside to dry before throwing them away.

A brush is a convenient way to spread oil over large surfaces and into carvings or mouldings.

Rub or brush a generous coating of oil into the wood grain. Leave it to soak in for 10 to 15 minutes, then wipe off excess oil with a clean cloth. After about six hours, coat the wood with oil once more. The next day, apply a third and final coat; raise a faint sheen by burnishing with a soft duster.

3

A
WHOLE
DAY

Making windows
burglarproof
50

Papering the ceiling
54

Painting the ceiling
56

Mending creaking stairs
58

Draughtproofing your doors
62

Sealing up draughty
windows
66

Putting up new shelving
68

Patching up damaged
plaster
74

Insulating your loft
78

Quick-and-easy double
glazing
81

Essential tools

Chisel

Drill bits

Hammer

Mallet

Marking gauge

Power drill

Screwdriver

Try square

MAKING WINDOWS BURGLARPROOF

Windows are a common means of entry for burglars – so make sure they are adequately secured, especially if they are on the ground floor or can be reached easily. There are all sorts of locks for wooden and metal windows, including some that lock automatically when you close the window. Locks for attaching to metal window frames are rather more difficult to fit, as you may have to cut threads for the screw fixings.

CHOOSING THE RIGHT LOCK

The type of lock suitable for a window depends on how the window opens. Sliding sashes are normally secured by locking them together, whereas casements – which open like doors – should be fastened to the outer window frame or locked by rendering the catches and stays immovable. Whichever type of lock you choose, it makes sense to buy the best you can afford for the more vulnerable windows and to spend less on ones that are especially difficult to reach.

Any window lock must be strong enough to resist forcing and has to be situated correctly for optimum security. On small windows, for example, fit a single lock as close as possible to the centre of the meeting rail or vertical stile; on larger windows, you will need two locks, spaced apart.

Locks that can only be released by a removable key are the most secure. Some keys will open any lock of the same design (an advantage in that you need fewer keys, although some burglars may carry a range of standard keys). With other locks, there will be several key variations.

Wooden windows need to be fairly substantial to accommodate mortise locks, so surface-mounted locks are often used. These are quite adequate and, being visible, act as a deterrent.

If the fixing screws are not concealed when the lock is in place, drill out the centre of the screws once fitted, so they cannot be withdrawn.

LOCKING A SASH WINDOW

There are two effective ways to prevent a forced entry through a sliding sash window. You can either use dual screws to immobilize both sashes or restrict their movement with sash stops.

Fitting dual screws

A dual screw consists of a bolt that passes through both meeting rails. The screw is operated by a special key, and there is little to see when the window is closed.

BOLT RECEIVERS   BOLT   KEY

1 To fit a dual screw, with the window shut and the catch engaged, drill through the inner meeting rail into the outer one. Wrap tape around the drill bit to gauge the depth accurately.

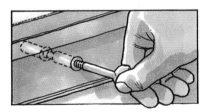

2 Slide the sashes apart and tap the two bolt-receiving devices into their respective holes. Close the window and insert the threaded bolt with the key until it is flush with the window frame. If need be, saw the bolt to length.

Installing sash stops

When the bolt is withdrawn with a key, a sash stop fitted to each side of a window allows it to be opened slightly for ventilation. As well as deterring burglars, sash stops prevent small children from opening the window any further.

1 To fit a stop, drill a hole in the upper sash for the bolt then screw the faceplate over it (on close-fitting sashes, you will probably have to recess the faceplate).

2 Screw the protective plate to the top edge of the lower sash to prevent the bolt bruising the wood.

Where to place window locks
The arrows indicate the best positions for window locks.

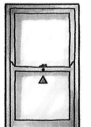

LOCKING A CASEMENT WINDOW

A locking bolt can be fitted to a wooden window frame: the bolt is engaged by turning a simple catch, but it can only be released with a removable key.

Fitting a surface-mounted casement lock
With the lock body screwed to the part of the window that opens, mark and cut a small mortise in the fixed frame for the bolt; then screw on the coverplate.

A similar device for metal windows is a clamp which, when fixed to the opening part of the casement, shoots a bolt that hooks over the fixed frame.

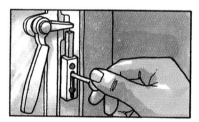

Locking the handle
A cockspur handle, which secures the opening edge of the casement to the fixed frame, can be locked by means of an extending bolt that you screw to the frame, just below the handle. However, ensure that the handle is not worn or loose – otherwise the lock may be ineffective.

Lockable handles, that will allow you to secure a window which is left ajar for ventilation, can be substituted in place of a standard handle.

LOCKING FANLIGHT WINDOWS

You can buy a variety of casement-type locks, as well as devices that secure the stay to the window frame. The simplest kind is screwed below the stay arm to receive a key-operated bolt passed through one of the holes in the stay arm. Purpose-made lockable stays are also available.

A better alternative is a device that clamps the window itself to the surrounding frame. Attach the lock first, then use it to position the staple.

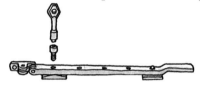

THIS TYPE OF LOCK BOLTS THE STAY TO THE WINDOW FRAME

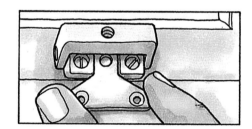

ATTACH THIS TYPE OF LOCK FIRST, THEN SCREW THE STAPLE TO THE FRAME

SECURING FRENCH WINDOWS WITH RACK BOLTS

French windows and other glazed doors are fairly easy to force open – a burglar only has to break a pane to reach the handle inside. Key-operated locks are essential to prevent a break-in.

Fit two rack bolts in the closing edge of a single glazed door. Locate one bolt near the top of the door, the other close to the bottom.

Each door of a double French window needs a bolt at the top and bottom, positioned so that one bolt shoots into the upper frame and the other into the threshold below. It is necessary to take each door off its hinges in order to fit the lower bolt.

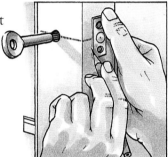

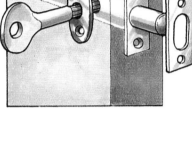

STANDARD
RACK BOLT
1 KEY
2 BARREL
3 KEYHOLE
  PLATE
4 LOCKING
  PLATE

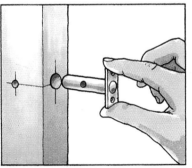

2 With the key holding the bolt in place, mark the recess for the faceplate; then pare out the recess with a chisel. Screw the bolt and keyhole plate to the door. Operate the bolt to mark the frame, then drill a 16mm (⅝in) diameter hole to a depth that matches the length of the bolt. Fit the locking plate over the hole.

1 Drill a hole – usually 16mm (⅝in) in diameter – for the barrel of the bolt in the edge of the door. Use a try square to transfer the centre of the hole to the inside face of the door. Mark the keyhole and drill it with a 10mm (⅜in) bit, then insert the bolt.

TIP ● ● ● ● ● ● ● ● ● ● ● ● ● ● ● ●

Locking sliding doors
If you have aluminium sliding doors, fit additional locks at the top and bottom to prevent the sliding frame from being lifted off its track. These locks are costly, but they offer at least a thousand key variations and provide good security.

Essential tools

Craft knife

Paperhanger's brush

Paste brush

Pasting table

Scissors

Seam roller

Tape measure

PAPERING THE CEILING

Papering a ceiling isn't as difficult as you may think: the techniques are basically the same as for papering a wall, except that the strips of paper are usually longer and more unwieldy to hold while you brush them into place. Set up a strong, secure work platform – it's virtually impossible to work from a single stepladder – and enlist a helper to support the folded paper while you position one end and progress backwards across the room. If you have marked out the ceiling first, the result should be faultless.

Marking out the ceiling

If possible, construct a work platform that spans the width of the room. The best type of platform to use is a purpose-made decorator's trestle, but you can manage with a pair of scaffold boards spanning two stepladders.

Now mark the ceiling to give a visual guide to positioning the strips of paper. Ideally, aim to work parallel with the window and away from the light, so you can see what you are doing and so that the light will not highlight the seams between strips. However, if the distance is shorter the other way, you may find it easier to hang the strips in that direction.

Mark a guide line along the ceiling, one roll width minus 12mm (½in) from the side wall, so that the first strip of paper will lap onto the wall.

See also:
Applying the paste, page 107

PUTTING UP THE PAPER

Paste the paper and fold it concertina-fashion. Drape the folded length over a spare roll and carry it to the work platform. You will find it easier if a helper supports the folded paper, leaving both your hands free for brushing it into place.

Hold the strip against the guide line, using a paperhanger's brush to stroke it onto the ceiling. Tap it into the wall angle, then gradually work backwards along the scaffold board, brushing on the paper as your helper unfolds it.

If the ceiling has a cornice, crease and trim the paper at the ends. Otherwise, allow the ceiling paper to lap the walls by 12mm (½in) so that it will be covered by the wallcovering. Work across the ceiling in the same way, butting the lengths of paper together. Cut the final strip roughly to width, and trim into the wall angle.

Papering a ceiling
The job is much easier if two people work together.

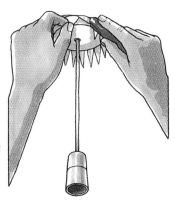

Cutting around a pendant light
Where the paper passes over a ceiling rose, cut several triangular flaps so you can pass the light fitting through the hole. Tap the paper all round the rose with a paperhanger's brush and continue on to the end of the length. Return to the rose and cut off the flaps with a knife.

Papering around a centrepiece
If your ceiling has a decorative plaster centrepiece, work out the position of the strips of paper so that one of the seams will pass through the middle. If you cut long flaps from the side of each strip, you can tuck the paper in all round the plaster moulding and cut the flaps off later.

Supporting pasted paper
If you have to work from a stepladder, your assistant can support the paper on a cardboard tube taped to a broom.

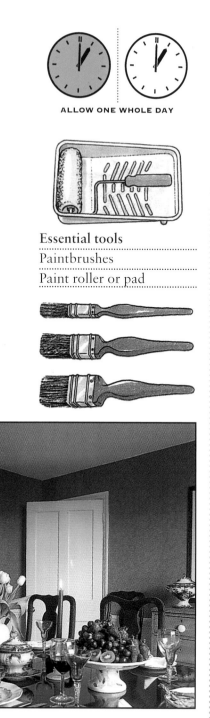

ALLOW ONE WHOLE DAY

Essential tools

Paintbrushes

Paint roller or pad

PAINTING THE CEILING

Even the most experienced decorator can't help dripping a little paint – so, unless you are planning to decorate the ceiling and walls of the room with the same colour paint, always paint the ceiling first. Cover the floor with dust sheets, and erect a work platform so you can cover as much of the surface as possible without changing position. For a first-class job, paper the ceiling with lining paper before you paint it.

A LIGHT CEILING CREATES A FEELING OF SPACE AND AIRINESS (ABOVE). DARK DRAMATIC TONES HAVE BEEN USED TO GREAT EFFECT (RIGHT), WHILE THE WHITE-PAINTED CORNICE ADDS LIGHT RELIEF AND DEFINES THE CEILING AREA.

See also:
Painting the living room, page 92
Papering the ceiling, page 54

APPLYING THE PAINT

Seal a dirty, stained ceiling with a general-purpose primer before you apply emulsion; cover heavy nicotine stains with an aluminium spirit-based sealer. You should bind powdery distemper to the ceiling with a white or clear stabilizing primer.

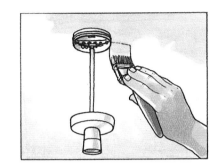

3 Switch off at the mains before unscrewing a ceiling-rose cover, since you will be exposing electrical connections. With the cover unscrewed, you can paint right up to the backplate with a small brush.

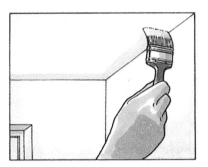

1 Start in a corner near the window and carefully paint along the edges with a small paintbrush. If you are going to paper the walls, brush paint well into the corners between walls and ceiling, covering the top 50mm (2in) of each wall.

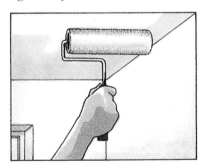

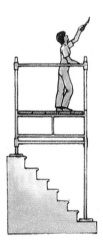

2 Working from the wet edges, paint in bands 600mm (2ft) wide, working away from the light. Whether you use a brush, pad or roller, apply each fresh load of paint just clear of the previous application, then blend in the junctions for even coverage.

If you are using conventional emulsion paint, you will need to apply a second coat to achieve an even coverage.

TIP ● ● ● ● ● ● ● ● ● ● ● ●

Reaching the ceiling
Painting a ceiling is far less tiring if you erect a work platform, using stepladders and planks (see page 54). Alternatively, hire slot-together scaffold frames to construct mobile platforms or fixed towers. Build a tower that compensates for the slope of the staircase when painting the ceiling above a stairwell.

Essential tools

Brace or power drill

Chisel

Countersink bit

Hammer

Mallet

Nail punch (nail set)

Plug cutter

Screwdriver

Tenon saw

Wood bits

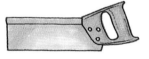

EXPOSED WOODEN STAIRS ARE VERY
ATTRACTIVE BUT IT IS IMPORTANT TO
CURE CREAKING AND FLEXING
PROBLEMS BEFORE YOU DISPENSE
WITH THE CUSHIONING AND
INSULATION BENEFITS PROVIDED
BY CARPET.

MENDING CREAKING STAIRS

A creaking staircase is an extremely irritating problem, caused by loose boards flexing and rubbing together. The most satisfactory repairs can be achieved by working from underneath the stairs, but if the underside of your staircase is plastered, it is simpler to work from above.

While you are working on the stairs, check the landings for loose floorboards.

WORKING FROM UNDERNEATH THE STAIRS

If it is possible to get to the underside of the staircase, have someone walk slowly up the stairs, counting them out loud. From your position under the stairs, note any loose steps and mark them with chalk. Have your assistant step on and off the ones you've marked while you inspect them to discover the source of the creaking.

Fixing a loose housing joint

If the end of a tread or riser (the vertical part of the step) is loose in its housing, the glued wedges that hold it in place may have worked loose.

1 *Prise out the loose wedges with a chisel. Clean the wedges with sandpaper or, if they are damaged, make new ones from hardwood.*

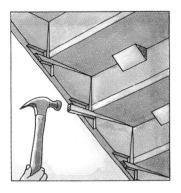

2 *Apply woodworking adhesive to the joints and tap the wedges home with a hammer.*

Replacing loose blocks

Check the triangular blocks that fit in the angle between the tread and riser. If the adhesive has failed on any of the faces, remove the blocks and clean off the old glue.

1 *Before replacing the blocks, prise the shoulder of the tread-to-riser joint slightly open with a chisel, apply new adhesive to it, then pull the joint up tight, using 38mm (1½in) countersunk screws.*

2 *Rub the glued blocks into the angle. If suction alone proves to be insufficient, use panel pins to hold the blocks in place while the adhesive sets (try to avoid treading on the repaired steps in the meantime). If some of the blocks are missing, cut new ones from a length of 50 x 50mm (2 x 2in) softwood.*

WORKING FROM ABOVE THE STAIRS

To identify where the problems occur, remove the stair carpet and walk slowly up the stairs. When you reach a creaking tread, shift your weight to and fro to discover which part is moving and mark it with chalk.

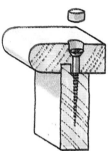

Screwing the nosing
A likely weakness will be the joint between the nosing (front edge of the tread) and the riser. This is normally a tongue-and-groove joint, or possibly a butt joint with a wooden moulding set into the angle between the two.
The easiest solution is to drill clearance holes for 38mm (1½in) countersunk screws directly over the centre line of the riser. Inject woodworking adhesive into the holes and work the joint a little to encourage the glue to spread into it, then pull the joint up tight with the screws. If the screws cannot be concealed by stair carpet, counterbore the holes to set the screw heads below the surface of the tread, then plug the holes with matching wood.

Gluing a loose riser joint
A loose joint at the back of the tread cannot be repaired easily from above. You can try working water-thinned PVA woodworking adhesive into the joint, but you cannot use woodscrews to pull the joint together.

As an alternative, reinforce the joint by gluing a section of 12 x 12mm (½ x ½in) triangular moulding into the angle between the tread and the riser – but for safety's sake don't make the depth of the tread less than 220mm (8¾in). Unless the stair carpet covers the full width of the treads, cut the moulding slightly shorter than the width of the carpet.

Another option is to glue a similar moulding to each step and apply a wood dye to unify the colour.

TIP ● ● ● ● ● ● ● ● ● ● ● ● ● ● ● ●
Curing squeaking floorboards
Over a period of time the flexing of the floor or expansion and contraction of the wood can loosen floorboard nails. The resulting movement of the wood against the nails or adjacent boards produces the annoying squeaks.

Use a nail punch (nail set) and hammer to drive the floorboard nails deeper; this allows the tapered edges of the nails to grip the wood firmly. If nails are missing, secure loose boards with ring-shank nails.

If nailing is not sufficient to hold a warped board in place, use countersunk woodscrews; dampening the wood thoroughly before fixing may help a board to 'give' as you screw it down. Bury the screw heads and cover them with plugs of wood if the floorboards are exposed.

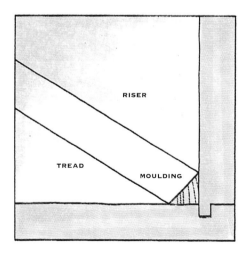

GLUING A LOOSE RISER JOINT

Essential tools

Hacksaw

Hammer

Power drill

Scissors

Screwdriver

Wood bits

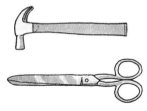

EXTERIOR DOORS ARE A NOTORIOUS
SOURCE OF HEAT LOSS AND THESE
SHOULD BE DRAUGHTPROOFED FIRST.
IN ADDITION TO THE EDGES AND THE
BOTTOM OF THE DOOR PAY
ATTENTION TO KEYHOLES AND
LETTERPLATES.

DRAUGHTPROOFING YOUR DOORS

Draughts account for quite a large proportion of the heat lost from your home and are also responsible for a good deal of discomfort. It is therefore worth spending a little money and effort to exclude them from your home. Locate draughts by running the flat of your hand along likely gaps. If you dampen your skin, it will enhance its sensitivity to the cold draughts. Otherwise, wait for a very windy day to conduct your search.

FILLING THE GAP BENEATH THE DOOR

If the gap between the door and floor is very large, it is bound to admit fierce draughts, so it pays to use a threshold excluder to seal the gap. If you fit an excluder to an exterior door, make sure it is suitable; and if you can't buy an excluder that fits the opening exactly, cut a longer one down to size.

Flexible-strip excluders
The simplest form of threshold excluder is a flexible strip of plastic or rubber that sweeps against the floorcovering to form a seal. The most basic versions are self-adhesive strips that are simply pressed along the bottom of the door, but other types have a rigid-plastic or aluminium extrusion screwed to the door to hold the strip in contact with the floor. This kind of excluder is rarely suitable for exterior doors and quickly wears out. However, it is inexpensive and easy to fit. Most types work best over smooth flooring.

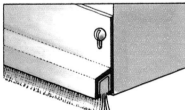

Brush seals
A long nylon-bristle brush set into either a metal or plastic extrusion can be used to exclude draughts under doors. This kind of excluder is suitable for slightly uneven or textured floorcoverings, and can be fitted to hinged or sliding doors.

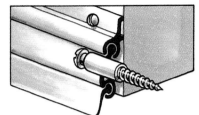

Automatic excluder
The plastic strip and its extruded clip are spring-loaded, so they lift from the floor as the door is opened. When you close the door, the excluder is pressed against the floor by a stop screwed to the doorframe. Suitable for both interior and exterior doors, automatic excluders inflict little wear on floorcoverings.

Flexible arch
The aluminium extrusion with its arched vinyl insert presses against the bottom edge of the door. As it has to be nailed or screwed to the floor, it is difficult to use a flexible-arch excluder on a solid-concrete floor. If you plan to fit one on an external door, buy a version that has additional underseals to prevent rain from seeping beneath it. You may have to plane the bottom of the door.

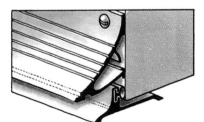

Door kits
The best solution for an exterior door is a kit combining an aluminium weather trim designed to shed rainwater, which is fitted to the door, and a weather bar with a tubular rubber or plastic draught excluder for screwing to the threshold.

Sealing around the door

A well-fitting door requires a gap of 2mm (¹⁄₁₆in) at top and sides so that it can be operated smoothly. However, a gap this large loses a great deal of heat. There are several ways to seal it, some of which are described here. The cheaper excluders have to be renewed regularly.

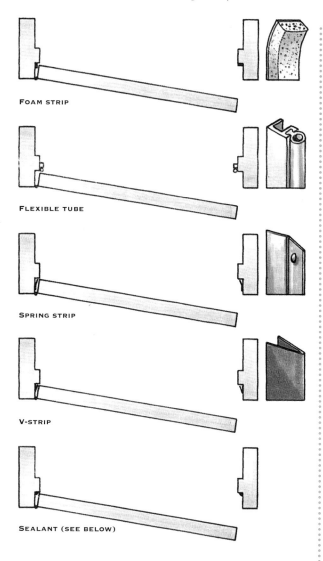

Foam strip

Flexible tube

Spring strip

V-strip

Sealant (see below)

FROM TOP TO BOTTOM

Stick-on foam strips
The most straightforward excluder is a self-adhesive foamed-plastic strip, which you stick around the rebate: the strip is compressed by the door, forming a seal. The cheapest polyurethane foam will be good for one or two seasons (although it's useless if painted), but is suitable for interior doors only. The better-quality vinyl-coated polyurethane, rubber or PVC foams are more durable and do not perish on exposure to sunlight, as their cheaper counterparts do. Don't stretch foam excluders when applying them, as that reduces their efficiency. The door may be difficult to close at first, but the excluder will adjust after a short period of use.

Flexible-tube excluders
A small vinyl tube held in a plastic or metal extrusion compresses to fill the gap around the door. The cheapest versions have an integrally moulded flange, which can be stapled to the doorframe, but they are not as neat.

Sprung-leaf strips
Thin metal or plastic strips that have a sprung leaf are either pinned or glued to the doorframe. The top and closing edges of the door brush past the sprung leaf, sealing the gap, while the hinged edge compresses a leaf on that side of the door. This type of draught excluder cannot cope with uneven surfaces unless a foam strip is incorporated on the flexible leaf.

V-strips
A variation on the sprung strip, the leaf is bent right back to form a V-shape. The strip can be mounted to fill the gap around the door or attached to the door stop so that the door closes against it. Most types are cheap and unobtrusive.

●●●●●●●●●●●●●●●●●●●●●●●● ● TIP

Draughtproofing sealant
You can effectively seal gaps with a bead of flexible sealant squeezed onto the door stop; a low-tack tape is applied to the surface of the door to act as a release agent. As the door is closed, it flattens the bead, filling the gap perfectly. When the sealant has set, the parting layer of tape is peeled from the door. You can also buy flexible tubing for bonding with sealant to compensate for movement.

DRAUGHT-PROOFING KEYHOLES AND LETTERBOXES

Make sure the external keyhole for a mortise lock is fitted with a pivoting coverplate to seal out draughts during the winter.

You can buy a hinged flap that screws onto the inner side of the door to cover a letter box. Some types have a brush seal mounted behind the flap to reduce draughts.

Keyhole coverplate
The coverplate is part of the escutcheon.

Brush-seal excluder
A brush seal neatly draughtproofs a letter box.

HAVING DRAUGHTPROOFED THE EXTERIOR DOORS, SEAL ONLY THOSE INTERIOR DOORS THAT CAUSE NOTICEABLE DRAUGHTS (THERE SHOULD BE SOME 'TRICKLE' VENTILATION FROM ROOM TO ROOM).

ALLOW ONE WHOLE DAY

Essential tools

Hacksaw

Hammer

Power drill

Scissors

Screwdriver

Wood bits

HINGED CASEMENT WINDOWS
(ABOVE) ARE EASY TO SEAL, USING
ANY OF THE EXCLUDERS SUGGESTED
FOR FITTING AROUND A DOOR; BUT
DRAUGHT-PROOFING A SLIDING SASH
WINDOW (RIGHT) PRESENTS A MORE
COMPLEX PROBLEM.

See also:
Draughtproofing doors, page 62

SEALING UP DRAUGHTY WINDOWS

Because they can affect every room in the house, draughty windows waste even more heat than a badly fitting door. As part of an energy-saving scheme, it is imperative to seal at least the worst offenders with effective draught excluders.

Draughtproofing a sash window

The top and bottom closing rails of a sash window can be sealed with any form of compressible excluder. The sliding edges usually admit fewer draughts, but they can be sealed with a brush seal fixed to the frame – inside for the lower sash, outside for the top one. A springy V-strip or a compressible plastic strip can be used to seal the gap between the sloping faces of the central meeting rails of a traditional sash window. For square rails, use a blade seal.

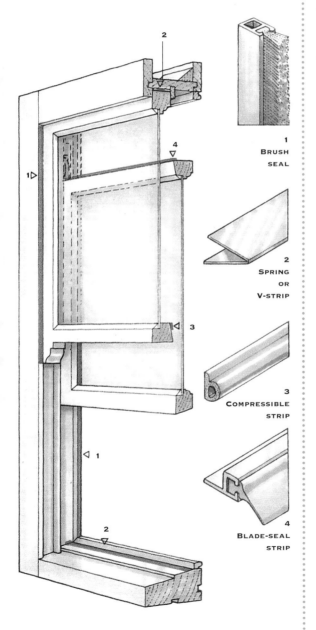

1
BRUSH
SEAL

2
SPRING
OR
V-STRIP

3
COMPRESSIBLE
STRIP

4
BLADE-SEAL
STRIP

Sealing a pivot window

When you close a pivot window, the movable frame comes to rest against fixed stops. Fitting excluders to these stops will seal off the worst of the draughts. You can use compressible spring or V-strip draughtproofing, or a good-quality flexible-tube strip, so long as they are weatherproof.

TIP ● ● ● ● ● ● ● ● ● ● ● ● ● ● ● ●

Filling large gaps

Large gaps left around newly fitted window frames (and doorframes) will be a source of draughts. Use an expanding-foam filler to seal these gaps. When the filler has set, repoint the masonry on the outside.

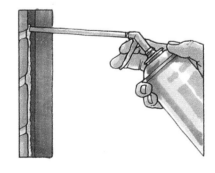

SEAL LARGE GAPS WITH EXPANDING FOAM

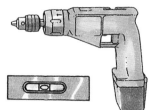

Essential tools

Hammer

Masonry bit

Plumb line

Power drill

Screwdriver

Spirit level

Tenon saw

Wood bits

IT SHOULD TAKE ABOUT A
DAY TO PUT UP A BANK
OF ADJUSTABLE SHELVES IN YOUR
LIVING ROOM OR IN A CHILD'S
BEDROOM.

PUTTING UP NEW SHELVING

Why is it that when you move into a new house or flat, there are never enough shelves for all your books or other possessions? And even when you think you have put up sufficient shelving for your future needs, the shelves always seem to be overflowing after just a couple of years. Thankfully, shelving is relatively inexpensive and easy to install.

Depending on where it is and what it is to be used for, shelving can be anything from a set of planks on functional-looking brackets in a garage to elegant spans of solid wood or plate glass on apparently delicate supports made of light alloy.

WHAT MATERIALS TO USE FOR YOUR SHELVES

Ready-cut shelves, in a wide variety of sizes, are usually made from solid wood or man-made boards, but shelves manufactured from glass or painted pressed steel are also available. Man-made-board shelves are painted or finished with wood or plastic veneer. If the standard range of shelves does not meet your requirements, you can make your own using the following materials.

Solid wood
Softwoods such as pine usually contain knots unless specially selected. Parana pine is generally knot-free and available in wide boards, but is more expensive.

You can buy hardwoods such as oak, beech and ash from some timber merchants, but their relatively high cost limits their use to special features and built-in furniture.

Blockboard
Blockboard is a stable man-made board constructed from strips of softwood glued and sandwiched between two layers of plywood-grade veneer.

The board is as strong as solid wood, provided the shelving is cut with the core running lengthways. You will need to lip the raw edges with veneer or solid wood to cover the core.

Plywood
Plywood is built up from veneers with their grain alternating at right angles to one another in order to provide strength and stability. The edges of plywood shelves can be left exposed or covered as for blockboard.

Chipboard
Chipboard, the cheapest man-made board, is most often used for the core of manufactured veneered shelving. Chipboard shelves are liable to bend under load unless they are supported properly.

Medium-density fibreboard
Medium-density fibreboard (MDF) is a dense and stable man-made board that is easy to cut and machine. It finishes smoothly on all edges and does not need to be lipped. MDF is ideal for painting or veneering.

Glass
Plate glass is an elegant material for display shelving. Use toughened glass, which is available to special order. Have it cut to size and the edges ground and polished by the supplier. Textured or wired glass can be used for added interest.

MAKING SURE YOUR SHELVES WON'T SAG

Solid timber or blockboard, with its core running lengthways, are best for sturdy shelving – but a shelf made from either material will still sag if its supports are too far apart. Veneered chipboard, though popular because of its low cost, availability and appearance, will eventually sag under relatively light loads, so it needs supporting at closer intervals than solid wood. Moving the supports in from each end of a shelf helps distribute the load and reduces the risk of sagging.

Material	Thickness	Light load	Medium load	Heavy load
Solid wood	18mm (¾in)	800mm (2ft 8in)	750mm (2ft 6in)	700mm (2ft 4in)
Blockboard	18mm (¾in)	800mm (2ft 8in)	750mm (2ft 6in)	700mm (2ft 4in)
Chipboard	16mm (⅝in)	750mm (2ft 6in)	600mm (2ft)	450mm (1ft 6in)
MDF	18mm (¾in)	800mm (2ft 8in)	750mm (2ft 6in)	700mm (2ft 4in)
Glass	6mm (¼in)	700mm(2ft 4in)	Not applicable	Not applicable

RECOMMENDED SHELF SPANS

The chart shows recommended maximum spans for shelves made from different materials. If you want to increase the length of any shelf, either move the supports closer together, add another bracket, use thicker material for the shelf, or stiffen its front edge.

Stiffening your shelves

Wooden battens, lippings or metal extrusions can be fixed to the underside or front edges of a shelf to increase its stiffness. A wall-fixed batten may also be used to support the back edge in some cases. A deep wooden front rail will conceal a strip-light fitting; a metal reinforcement can be slimmer and less noticeable.

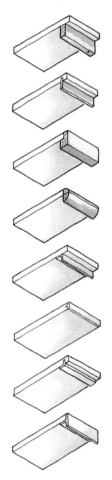

FROM TOP TO BOTTOM
WOODEN BATTEN
PLYWOOD STRIP
REBATED BATTEN
HALF-ROUND LIPPING
SCREWED METAL ANGLE
GROOVED METAL T-SECTION
GROOVED METAL ANGLE
SCREWED METAL T-SECTION

CHOOSING THE BEST SHELF-SUPPORT SYSTEM

The method you use to support a bank of shelving depends a great deal on your chosen location. It is often possible, for example, to span a fireside alcove with fixed built-in shelves that have no apparent means of support. Adjustable shelf brackets offer a greater degree of flexibility, allowing you to redesign your storage system at some time in the future as your collection or library expands. Furthermore, this type of shelving does not rely on side walls for support and can be cantilevered off a straight wall. The brackets may be made from pressed, cast or wrought steel, or from extruded alloy.

Shelf brackets

There are many systems on the market with brackets which slot or clip into metal upright supports that are screwed to the wall. Most uprights have holes or slots at close intervals that accommodate lugs on the rear of each bracket. In one system the upright has a continuous groove over its entire length, so that the brackets may be placed at any level.

One advantage of such systems is that the weight and stress of loaded shelves are distributed down the supporting uprights. Another factor in their favour is that, once the uprights are in place, shelving arrangements can be changed easily and further shelves added, as the need arises, without the necessity for more fixings.

Use the cheap and functional pressed-metal types for utilitarian shelving in a garage or workshop, and choose the more expensive and attractive brackets for your storage needs around the house.

Built-in shelves

Made-to-measure shelving tends to look more substantial and permanent than even the best bracket system. However, it invariably means more work, since you have to cut and fit each shelf individually. You must also make your own supports, usually battens screwed to the walls or vertical side panels made from solid wood or man-made boards. And unless you incorporate a library-style adjustable system, built-in shelves tend to be fixed and therefore less adaptable for future needs.

FIXED PRESSED-
STEEL BRACKETS

ADJUSTABLE BRACKET
WITH SLOTTED UPRIGHT

ADJUSTABLE BRACKET
WITH GROOVED UPRIGHT

PUTTING UP WALL-MOUNTED SHELVING

The construction of the walls will to some extent determine the type of fixing and the positioning of your shelves. On masonry walls, for example, you can place shelf supports almost anywhere; on a timber-framed wall shelves should ideally be fixed to the studs or noggings, but you can use special cavity fixings provided the loads are not excessive.

Loads cantilevered from wall brackets impose great stress on the fixing screws, especially the top ones. If the screws are too small, or if the wall plugs are inadequate, the fixing may be torn out. This is even more likely when you are erecting deep shelves. The fixings for a built-in shelf, with its ends supported on battens within a masonry alcove, are not so highly stressed.

For most ordinary shelving, brackets fixed to a wall of masonry with 50mm

(2in) screws and wall plugs should be adequate. Deep shelves intended for a heavy load such as a television set or stack of records may need more robust fixings such as wall bolts, though extra brackets to prevent the shelf sagging will also share the weight. Brackets must be long enough to support almost the entire depth of a shelf.

Fixing individual shelf brackets
When fixing pairs of individual brackets to a solid wall, first mark two vertical guide lines. Hold one bracket at the required height and mark the wall through the fixing holes.

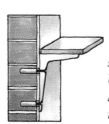

1 Drill into the wall with a masonry bit, insert wall plugs and screw the bracket in place. Using one of the shelves and a spirit level, position the second bracket, then mark and fix it similarly.

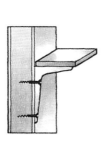

2 When fixing brackets to a timber-framed wall, locate the studs and drill pilot holes for the screws. Lightly lubricate screws that are difficult to insert. If you use cavity-wall fixings, drill adequate clearance holes through the plaster lining in order to insert the fittings.

When you are erecting a bank of shelving, fix all the brackets first and simply place the shelves on them. Use a plumb line or spirit level to align the ends of the shelves before you fix them to the brackets.

Fitting a shelving system

Strong wall fixings are essential, since even one loose upright could jeopardize the safety of the whole bank of shelving.

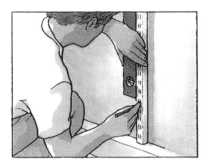

1 The upright supports must be vertical, and the best way of ensuring this is to fix each one lightly to the wall by its top screw, then, holding it vertical with the aid of a spirit level, mark the position of the bottom screw.

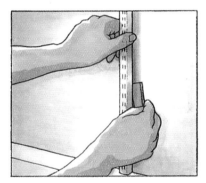

2 With that screw in place, you can check that the upright is vertical in its other plane, not sloping outwards because the wall is out of true. If required, place packing behind the upright to correct it. Also insert packing wherever hollows occur close to fixing points.

Clip one bracket to the upright, then another to the second upright while you hold it against the wall. Get a helper to lay a shelf across the brackets, then use a spirit level to check that the shelf is horizontal.

Mark the top hole of the second upright, and fix that upright as you did the first one. Locate brackets in both uprights and fix the shelves to them. A gap between the back of the shelves and the wall may provide a useful space for cables leading to lamps or equipment.

Making built-in shelves

The simplest way to make built-in open shelves is to fit them into alcoves such as those flanking a chimney breast. However, the surface of the walls is unlikely to be perfectly regular, and some trimming of the shelves may be needed to make them a good fit. Mark the height of the shelves and draw levelled lines from the marks, using a spirit level. Cut wooden support battens to suit the depth of the shelves.

If the shelves are not fitted with a deep lipping, cut the front ends of the supports to a 45-degree angle; you will hardly notice them once you have filled the shelves with books or other items.

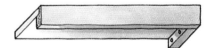

For a better appearance, apply deep lippings to the front edges of the shelves. These make the shelving look more substantial and hide the supports.

For a more refined look, make your shelf supports from L-section metal extrusion. Fix the supports securely to the wall with countersunk screws.

ALLOW ONE WHOLE DAY

Essential tools

Bolster chisel

Filling knife

Hammer

Paintbrush

Plasterer's trowel

Tinsnips

Wallpaper scraper

PATCHING UP DAMAGED PLASTER

Whatever you intend to use as a decorative finish, plastered walls or ceilings must be made good by filling cracks and holes. Patching plasterwork can be a messy job and if you are not careful you can end up with white footprints all round the house. Cover the floor around the work area with dust sheets, particularly if you are unable to remove the carpets. If you are working overhead also cover the furniture. You don't need to be an expert plasterer unless you are faced with repairing large areas of loose plaster, in which case it is worth hiring a professional. There are easy-to-use fine fillers available, but if you need to make good a thick coating you can use the traditional undercoat and top-coat plasters or one of the newer one-coat plasters. Let plaster and fillers dry out thoroughly before you begin to apply paint or wallcoverings.

TIP

Levelling the repair

Uneven plaster can spoil any decorative finish. Use a straight-edged batten to help level the surface of a plaster patch before finishing with a trowel.

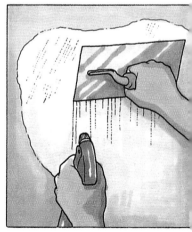

LEVEL THE REPAIR WITH A BATTEN THEN SMOOTH OFF WITH A TROWEL. SPRAY PLASTER OCCASIONALLY AS YOU SMOOTH IT.

FILLING CRACKS AND HOLES

Special flexible emulsions and textured paints are designed to cover hairline cracks, but larger ones will reappear in a relatively short time if they are not filled adequately.

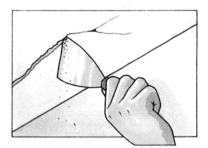

1 Rake loose material from a crack with the blade of a scraper or filling knife. Undercut the edges of larger cracks in order to provide a key for the filling. Mix up interior-grade cellulose filler to a stiff consistency or use a pre-mixed filler.

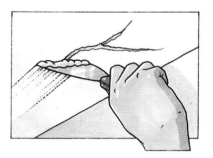

2 Dampen the crack with a paintbrush, then press the filler in with a filling knife. Drag the blade across the crack to force the filler in, then draw it along the crack to smooth the filler. Leave the filler standing slightly proud of the surface, ready for sanding flush with abrasive paper. Fill shallow cracks in one go; but build up the filler in stages in deep cracks, letting each application set before adding more.

Fill and rub down small holes and dents in solid plasterwork, using the methods recommended for filling cracks.

TIP ● ● ● ● ● ● ● ● ● ● ● ● ● ● ● ● ● ● ●

Gaps between skirting boards
Large gaps can open up between your skirting boards and the wall plaster. Cellulose filler simply falls into the cavity behind, so bridge the gap with a roll of press-in-place butyl sealant.

PATCHING UP DAMAGED CORNERS
Cracks sometimes appear in the corner between walls or between the wall and ceiling; fill these by running your finger dipped in filler along the crack. When the filler has hardened, rub it down with medium-grade abrasive paper.

1 To build up a chipped external corner, dampen the plaster and use a filling knife to scrape the filler onto the damaged edge, working from both sides of the corner.

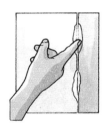

2 Let the filler stiffen, then shape it with a wet finger until it closely resembles the original profile. When the filler is dry, smooth it with abrasive paper.

PATCHING A LATH-AND-PLASTER WALL

FILLING HOLES IN PLASTER-BOARD

If you live in an older house, you might find that a wall between two rooms is hollow. This type of partition wall is made with a timber framework covered with thin strips of wood known as laths which serve as a base for the plaster. If the laths are intact, just fill any holes in the plaster with cellulose filler or fresh plaster. If some laths are broken, you need to reinforce the repair with a piece of fine expanded-metal mesh.

Use plasterer's glass-fibre patching tape when mending holes up to about 75mm (3in) across.

1 Stick on the self-adhesive strips in a star shape over the hole, then apply cellulose filler and feather the edges.

2 Alternatively, use an offcut of plasterboard just larger than the hole yet narrow enough to slot through. Bore a hole in the middle and thread a length of string through. Tie a galvanized nail to one end of the string.

3 Butter the ends of the offcut with filler, then feed it into the hole. Pull on the string to force it against the back of the cladding, then press filler into the hole so that it is not quite flush with the surface. When the filler is hard, cut off the string and apply a thin coat of filler for a flush finish.

1 Rake out loose plaster and undercut the edge of the hole with a bolster chisel. Use tinsnips to cut the metal mesh to the shape of the hole, but a little larger.

2 The mesh is flexible, so you can easily bend it in order to tuck the edge behind the sound plaster all round.

3 Flatten the mesh against the laths with light taps from a hammer and, if possible, staple the mesh to a wall stud to hold it.

4 Apply one thin coat of backing plaster and let it dry for about an hour before you fill the hole flush with more plaster.

PATCHING LARGER HOLES

A large hole punched through a plasterboard wall or ceiling cannot be patched with wet plaster only.

1 Using a sharp craft knife and a straightedge, cut back the damaged board to the nearest studs or joists at each side of the hole. Cut a new panel of plasterboard to fit snugly within the hole and nail it to the joists or studs using galvanized plasterboard nails.

2 Use a steel plasterer's trowel to spread finish plaster over the panel, forcing it well into the edges. Allow the plaster to stiffen, then smooth it with a dry trowel. You may have to add another layer to bring the patch to the level of the wall or ceiling.

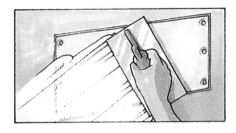

PLASTER AND PLASTERBOARD SURFACES ARE FAIRLY TOUGH, BUT VULNERABLE AREAS SUCH AS SLOPING CEILINGS, ALCOVES AND EXTERNAL CORNERS CAN SUFFER DAMAGE.

STEEL PLASTERER'S TROWEL

ALLOW ONE WHOLE DAY

Essential tools

For blanket insulation:

Large pair of scissors

Sharp kitchen knife

For loose-fill insulation:

Broom

Hammer

Home-made spreader

Scissors

Screwdriver

Check roof timbers for woodworm

Woodworm is the common name for a variety of woodboring insects. Familiar species are the deathwatch beetle (top) and the furniture beetle (below).

See also:
Lagging your pipes, page 20

INSULATING YOUR LOFT

Approximately a quarter of the heat lost from an average house goes through the roof, so preventing this should be one of your priorities when it comes to insulating your home. Provided that you are able to gain access to your loft space, reducing heat loss through the roof is simply a matter of laying insulating material between the joists, which is cheap, quick and effective.

On inspection, you may find that your roof space has existing but inadequate insulation – at one time even 25mm (1in) of insulation was considered to be acceptable. It is worth installing extra material to bring the insulation up to the recommended thickness of 150mm (6in).

GETTING READY

Check roof timbers for woodworm or signs of rot, so they can be treated first. Make sure that all the electrical wiring is sound, and lift it clear so that you can lay insulation beneath it.

The plaster or plasterboard ceiling below will not support your weight. You therefore need to lay a plank or two, or a chipboard panel, across the joists so you can move about safely.

If there is no permanent lighting in the loft, rig up an inspection lamp on an extension lead and move it wherever it is needed – or hang the lamp high up to provide an overall light.

Most attics are very dusty, so wear old clothes and a gauze face mask. It is also wise to wear protective gloves, especially if you're handling glass-fibre batts or blanket insulation, which may irritate sensitive skin.

LAYING BLANKET INSULATION

Blanket insulation is made from glass fibre, mineral fibre or rock fibre – it is widely available in the form of rolls that fit snugly between the joists. Before starting to lay blanket insulation, seal gaps around pipes, vents or wiring entering the loft with flexible mastic.

Remove the blanket wrapping in the loft (the insulation is compressed for storage and transportation, but swells to its true thickness when released).

Begin by placing one end of a roll into the eaves – make sure you don't cover the ventilation gap (trim the end of the blanket to a wedge shape so that it does not obstruct the airflow).

Unroll the blanket between the joists, pressing it down to form a snug fit – but don't compress it. If you have bought a roll that's slightly wider than the joist spacing,

allow it to curl up against the timbers on each side.

Continue at the opposite side of the loft with another roll. Cut it to butt up against the end of the first one, using either a large kitchen knife or a pair of long-bladed scissors. Continue across the loft till all the spaces are filled. Trim the insulation to fit odd spaces.

Do not cover the casings of light fittings that protrude into the loft space. Also, avoid covering electrical cables in case they overheat – lay the cables on top of the blanket or clip them to the sides of the joists above it.

Do not insulate the area immediately below a cold-water cistern (the heat rising from the room below will help to prevent freezing during the winter).

Cut a piece of blanket to fit the cover of the entrance hatch, and attach it with PVA adhesive or with cloth tapes and drawing pins. Fit foam draught excluder around the edges of the hatch.

Insulating with glass-fibre blanket
Place the end of a roll against the eaves and trim at an angle (1) or fit eaves vents (2). Lay rolls between joists (3), and trim ends to fit with scissors (4). Clip cables to joists (5) or lay them over the blankets. Don't place insulation below a cistern. Insulate cistern and cold-water pipes separately.

LAYING LOOSE-FILL INSULATION

Loose-fill insulation in either pellet or granular form is poured between the joists, up to the recommended depth of 150mm (6in). Exfoliated vermiculite, made from the mineral mica, is the most common form of loose-fill insulation on the market – but other types, such as mineral wool, cork granules and cellulose fibre, are also available. Run electrical cable over the insulation or along the joists as suggested for glass-fibre blankets.

Seal all gaps around pipes and vents to prevent condensation.

When laying loose-fill insulation, to avoid blocking the eaves, wedge strips of plywood or thick cardboard between the joists, or install proprietary eaves vents as recommended for blanket insulation.

Pour insulation onto the ceiling and distribute it roughly with a broom. Level it with a spreader cut from hardboard. If the joists are shallow, nail on lengths of wood to build up their height to at least 150mm (6in), if only to support walkway boarding in specific areas of the loft.

Cover cold-water pipes with cardboard before pouring insulation.

To insulate the entrance hatch, screw battens around the outer edge of the cover, then fill with granules and pin on a hardboard lid to contain them.

Lagging cold-water cisterns

To comply with current bylaws, your cold-water-storage cistern must be insulated. Buy a Bylaw 30 kit, which includes a jacket and all the other equipment that is required. Insulate your central-heating expansion tank at the same time.

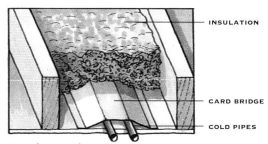

INSULATION

CARD BRIDGE

COLD PIPES

Insulating the pipes

If there are cold-water pipes running between the joists, lay blanket insulation over them to prevent them from freezing. If that is not practical, insulate each pipe run separately with foamed-plastic tubes.

Before pouring loose-fill insulation, lay a bridge made from thin card over cold-water pipes running between the joists, so they will benefit from warmth rising from the room below. If the joists are shallow, cover the pipes with foam tubes before pouring the insulation.

Spreading loose-fill insulant

Seal gaps around pipes and vents (1). Use strips of plywood to prevent insulant from blocking ventilation (2), or fit eaves vents. Use a spreader to level the insulant (3), having covered pipes with a cardboard bridge (4). Insulate and draughtproof the hatch cover (5).

QUICK-AND-EASY DOUBLE GLAZING

There are a great many different secondary glazing systems on the market, but by far the simplest and cheapest employs a sheet of thin, flexible plastic film taped across the window frame. It makes surprisingly effective double glazing and can be removed at the end of the winter. Taped film is safe because it can be cut away easily in an emergency.

Covering the window with film

Film taped to the movable sash will reduce heat loss through the glass and provide accessible ventilation, but it won't stop draughts. Film stretched right across the window frame has the advantage of cutting down heat loss and eliminating draughts at the same time.

ALLOW ONE WHOLE DAY

Stretching the film across a single window takes perhaps half an hour, but you may need most of the day to 'double-glaze' your whole house.

Essential tools

Craft knife

Hairdryer

Scissors

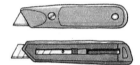

1 Clean the window frame and cut the plastic roughly to size, allowing an overlap all round. Apply double-sided tape to the edges of the frame, then peel off the backing paper.

2 Attach the plastic film to the top rail, then tension it onto the tape on the sides and bottom of the window frame. Apply only light pressure until you have positioned the film, and then rub it down onto the tape all round.

3 Remove all creases and wrinkles in the film, using a hair dryer set to a high temperature. Starting at an upper corner, move the dryer slowly across the film, holding it about 6mm (¼in) from the surface.

4 When the film is taut, cut off the excess plastic with a knife.

81

4

THE
COMPLETE
WEEKEND

Laying a small patio
84
Making a real-stone
pathway
90
Painting the living room
92
Refurbishing your kitchen
cabinets
102
Papering the spare room
104
Blocking out noisy
neighbours
114
Tiling the bathroom
117

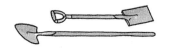

Essential tools

Angle grinder

Bolster chisel

Club hammer

Face mask

Hose or watering can

Garden roller

Goggles

Handbrush or broom

Rake

Spade

Spirit level

Straightedge

Trowel

Shapes and sizes

There is a fairly standard range of shapes and modular sizes of paving available. Although it is possible to carry most slabs single-handed, it is advisable to have help when moving large slabs or heavy natural stones into place.

LAYING A SMALL PATIO

A small paved area surrounded by attractive shrubs and low planting makes a perfect suntrap for relaxing in the garden. Provided you are not too ambitious, it is also relatively easy to achieve, using cast-concrete paving slabs available from any large DIY store or garden centre. The slabs are made by hydraulic pressing or casting in moulds to create the desired surface finish. Pigments and selected aggregates added to the concrete mix create the illusion of natural stone or a range of muted colours.

Laying heavy paving slabs involves a good deal of physical labour, but in terms of technique it is no more complicated than tiling a wall. Accurate setting out and careful laying, especially during the early stages, will produce perfect results.

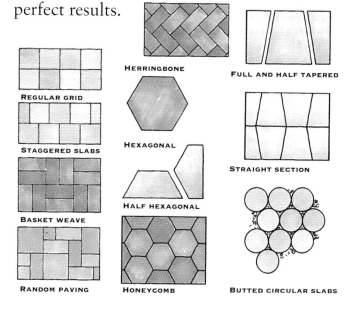

REGULAR GRID

STAGGERED SLABS

BASKET WEAVE

RANDOM PAVING

HERRINGBONE

HEXAGONAL

HALF HEXAGONAL

HONEYCOMB

FULL AND HALF TAPERED

STRAIGHT SECTION

BUTTED CIRCULAR SLABS

PLANNING THE AREA

To eliminate the task of cutting paving slabs to fit, try to plan an area of paving to be laid with whole slabs only. If the patio is to be laid next to your house, take your measurements from a convenient wall, or allow for a 100 to 150mm (4 to 6in) margin of gravel between the paving and wall. A gravel margin not only saves time and money by using fewer slabs, but also provides an area for planting climbers and for adequate drainage to keep the wall dry. Even so, allow for a 16mm per metre (⅝in per yard) slope across the paving, so that most surface water will drain into the garden. Any paving must be 150mm (6in) below the damp-proof course to protect the building.

Allowing for the joints

As paving slabs are made to fairly precise dimensions, marking out an area simply involves accurate measurement, allowing for a 6 to 8mm (¼in) gap between slabs. Some slabs are cast with sloping edges to provide a tapered joint, and these should be butted edge to edge. Use pegs and string to mark out the perimeter of the paved area, and check your measurements before you start work.

BUTT SLOPING EDGES
TOGETHER TO MAKE
A TAPERED JOINT

PREPARING A SOUND BASE FOR THE PAVING

Paving slabs must be laid upon a firm, level base, but the depth and substance of that base depends on the type of soil and the proposed use of the paving.

For small areas and light loads

For a small patio, remove grass and topsoil to allow for the thickness of the slabs, plus a 25mm (1in) layer of sharp sand and an extra 18mm (¾in) so that the paving will be below the level of surrounding turf and thus will not damage your lawn mower. Compact the soil with a garden roller, spread the sand with a rake, and level it by scraping and tamping with a length of timber.

LEVEL THE SAND BASE
WITH A STRAIGHTEDGE

FOR CLAY OR PEAT SOILS ● ● ● ● ●

To support heavier loads, or if the soil is composed of clay or peat, lay a sub-base of firmly compacted hardcore (broken bricks or crushed stone) to a depth of 75 to 100mm (3 to 4in) before spreading the sand to level the surface.

If you are planning to park vehicles on the paving, increase the depth of the hardcore to 150mm (6in).

LAYING THE PAVING SLABS

Once you have laid your base, set up the string lines again as a guide for laying the edging slabs on the sand. Work in both directions from a corner. When you are satisfied with their positions, lift the slabs one at a time and set them on a bed of mortar (1 part cement : 4 parts builder's sand). Add just enough water to make a firm mortar.

1 *Lay a fist-size blob of mortar under each corner, and one more to support the centre of the slab. If you intend to drive vehicles across the slabs, lay a continuous bed of mortar about 50mm (2in) thick.*

2 *Lay three slabs at a time with 6mm (¼in) wooden spacers between. Level each slab by tapping with a heavy hammer, using a block of wood to protect the slab. Check the alignment with a straightedge.*

3 *Gauge the slope across the paving by setting up datum pegs along the high side. Drive them into the ground until the top of each corresponds to the finished surface of the paving, then use the straightedge to check the fall on the slabs. Lay the remainder of the slabs, working out from the corner each time to keep the joints square. Remove the spacers before the mortar sets.*

Don't walk on the paving for two to three days, until the mortar has set. If you have to cross the area, lay planks across the slabs to spread the load.

4 *To fill the gaps between the slabs, brush a dry mortar mix of 1 part cement : 3 parts builder's sand into the open joints. Remove any surplus material from the surface of the paving, then sprinkle the area with a very fine spray of water to consolidate the mortar. Avoid dry mortaring if heavy rain is imminent; it may wash the mortar out.*

CUTTING SLABS TO FIT NARROW MARGINS

Sometimes it is impossible to plan an area of paving without having to use cut slabs to fill a border or to fit around immovable obstructions.

When cutting paving slabs with a chisel or an angle grinder, always protect your eyes with plastic goggles. An angle grinder throws up a great deal of dust, so wear a simple gauze face mask, too, as a safeguard.

2 Lay the slab on a bed of sand and place a block of wood at one end of the groove. Strike the block with a hammer while moving it along the groove until the slab splits. Clean up the edge with a bolster.

1 Mark a line across the slab with a soft pencil or chalk. Using a bolster and hammer, chisel a groove about 3mm (⅛in) deep along the line. Continue the groove down both edges and across the underside of the slab.

● ● ● **TIP**
A perfect cut
For a perfect cut, hire an angle grinder fitted with a stone-cutting disc. Using the grinder, score a deep groove as before. Tap along the groove with a bolster until the slab splits.

SLAB COLOURS AND TEXTURES

THE RANDOM, REAL YORKSTONE PATH (ABOVE), HAS OPEN, UNPOINTED JOINTS, THIS ALLOWS FOLIAGE TO GROW BETWEEN THE STONES.

A MORE FORMAL PATIO (RIGHT) OF PRECAST SLABS MAKES AN IDEAL LEVEL SEATING AREA.

CLAY PAVING BRICKS EDGED WITH GRANITE SETS (BELOW) PROVIDE A LABOUR-SAVING ALTERNATIVE TO THE CONVENTIONAL GARDEN LAWN.

Essential tools

Bolster

Broom

Club hammer

Goggles

Mallet

Old paintbrush

Spirit level

Straightedge

Trowel

MAKING A REAL-STONE PATHWAY

The informal nature of paths or patios laid with irregular-shaped paving stones has always been popular. The random effect, which many people find more appealing than the geometric symmetry of neatly laid slabs, is also less taxing to achieve. A good eye for shape and proportion is more important than a practised technique.

Choosing your materials

Use broken concrete slabs if you can find enough of them, but in terms of appearance nothing compares with natural rock, which splits into thin layers of its own accord as it is quarried. Random broken stone is also ideal for paving and can be obtained at a very reasonable price if you can collect it yourself.

BROKEN PAVING SLABS (ABOVE) CAN MAKE ATTRACTIVE PAVING BUT NOTHING CAN BEAT THE LOOK OF NATURAL STONE AS SHOWN IN THE PATHWAY MADE OF RANDOM BROKEN LIMESTONE (RIGHT).

LAYING THE STONES

You can set out string lines to define straight edges for stone paving, although they will never be as precisely defined as those formed with regular cast-concrete slabs.

Arrange an area of stones, selecting them for a close fit but avoiding too many straight, continuous joints. Trim those that don't quite fit with a bolster and hammer. Reserve larger stones for the perimeter of the paved area, as small stones tend to break away.

1 Use a mallet or block of wood and a hammer to bed each stone into the sand until they are all perfectly stable and reasonably level.

2 Having bedded an area of about 1sq m (1sq yd), use a straightedge and spirit level to true up the stones. If necessary, add or remove sand beneath individual stones until the area is level.

3 When the main area is complete, fill in the larger gaps with small stones, tapping them into place with a mallet.

4 Fill the joints by spreading more sand across the paving and sweeping it into the joints from all directions. Alternatively, mix up a stiff, almost dry, mortar and press it into the joints with a trowel, leaving no gaps.

Use an old paintbrush to smooth the mortared joints, and wipe the stones clean with a damp sponge.

ALLOW THE COMPLETE WEEKEND

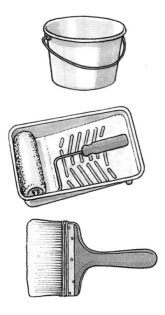

Essential tools

For painting walls:

50mm (2in) paintbrush

150mm (6in) paintbrush

or paint roller

For painting woodwork:

12, 25 and 50mm (½, 1 and 2in) paintbrushes

Paint kettle

Sharp scraping blade

See also:
Painting the ceiling, page 56
Papering the ceiling, page 54
Patching up
damaged plaster, page 74
Stripping old wallpaper, page 44

PAINTING THE LIVING ROOM

Completing even a small room in a single weekend can be difficult if you use solvent-based paints, because they must be left to dry thoroughly before you apply subsequent coats. Provided you have painted or papered the ceiling and prepared the walls the previous weekend, you should be able to apply two coats of emulsion to the walls in one day, so long as you get started reasonably early. If on the second day you are running out of time, try to leave the work at a stage where you can finish painting over a couple of evenings or the next weekend.

However, if you really need to finish the job quickly, use fast-drying acrylic paints and water-based primers, or consider using one-coat paints which eliminate the need for undercoats.

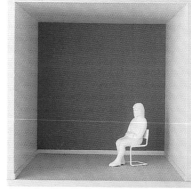

WARM COLOURS APPEAR TO ADVANCE

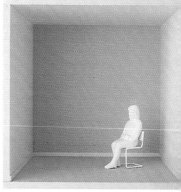

A COOL COLOUR OR PALE TONE RECEDES

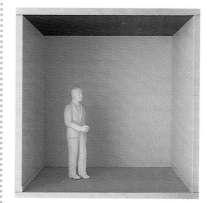

A DARK CEILING WILL APPEAR LOWER

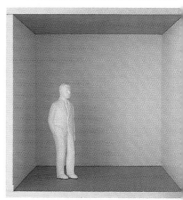

DARK SURFACES MAKE A ROOM SMALLER

92

STARTING WITH THE WALLS

Cover the floor with dust sheets and erect a safe work platform, so you can reach the top of a wall and cover as much of it as possible. You will complete the job in much less time and achieve better results if you don't have to keep moving a stepladder.

Choosing the paint

Emulsion paint is most people's first choice for decorating indoors: it is relatively cheap, practically odourless, and there are several qualities of paint to suit different circumstances.

Vinyl emulsions are the most popular and practical paints for walls and ceilings. They are available in liquid or thixotropic (non-drip) consistencies, with matt or satin (semi-gloss) finishes. You will need to apply two coats of standard emulsion to avoid a patchy, uneven appearance, perhaps thinning the first coat slightly when painting porous surfaces.

A one-coat, high-opacity emulsion is intended to save you time, but you will not get satisfactory results if you try to apply it too thinly, especially when overpainting strong colours.

New-plaster emulsions are specially formulated for new interior walls and ceilings, to allow moisture vapour to escape; standard vinyl emulsions are not sufficiently permeable.

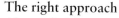

The right approach

Always finish a complete wall before you take a break, otherwise a change of tone may show between two sections painted at different times.

1 Use a small brush to paint the edges, starting at a top corner of the room. If you are right-handed, work from right to left, and vice versa.

2 Using a wide brush or roller, apply emulsion paint to cover an area of about 600 to 900mm (2 to 3ft) square at a time, working in horizontal bands across the room. If you prefer to use a solvent-based paint, brush on the finish in vertical bands as shown.

PAINTING WITH BRUSHES

A brush about 200mm (8in) wide will cover an area quickly, but if you are not used to handling a large brush, your wrist will soon tire; you may find a 150mm (6in) brush more comfortable to use, even though the job will take a little longer. You will also need a 50mm (2in) brush for the edges and corners.

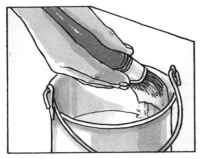

1 Don't overload a brush with paint; it leads to messy work, and ruins the bristles if the paint is allowed to dry in the roots. Dip no more than the first third of the brush into the paint, wiping off excess on the side of the container to prevent drips. When using thixotropic paint, load the brush and apply paint without removing excess.

2 You can hold the brush whichever way feels comfortable to you, but the 'pen' grip is the most versatile, enabling your wrist to move the brush freely in any direction. Hold the brush handle between your thumb and forefinger, with your fingers on the ferrule (metal band) and your thumb supporting it from the other side. Apply the paint in vertical strokes, then spread it at right angles to even out the coverage.

PAINTING WITH A ROLLER

A paint roller with interchangeable sleeves is an excellent tool for applying paint to large areas. Choose a roller about 225mm (9in) long for painting walls. Larger ones are available, but they become tiring to use.

There are a number of different sleeves to suit the type of paint and texture of the surface. Long-haired sheepskin and synthetic-fibre sleeves are the most practical for textured surfaces, especially when applying emulsion paint.

1 You will need a special paint tray to load a standard roller. Having dipped the sleeve lightly into the paint reservoir, roll it gently onto the ribbed part of the tray to coat the roller evenly.

2 Use zig-zag strokes with the roller, painting the surface in all directions to achieve an even coverage. Keep the roller on the surface at all times: if you let it spin at the end of a stroke, it will spatter paint onto the floor or adjacent surfaces.

If you are using solvent-based paints, plan to decorate windows early in the day to make sure the paint will be dry enough to close the windows by nightfall. Finish with the skirting boards, in case you touch the floor with the brush and specks of dust get transferred to other areas. As a precaution, slide strips of thin card under the skirting to act as a paint shield (don't use newspaper; it will tear and remain stuck to the skirting).

Using solvent-based paints

The familiar solvent-based paints (oil paints) are available as high-gloss and satin finishes, with both liquid and thixotropic consistencies. Indoors, they last for years with only the occasional wash down to remove finger marks. One or two undercoats are essential.

A one-coat paint, with its creamy consistency and high-pigment content, can protect primed wood and obliterate existing colours without undercoating. Apply it liberally and allow it to flow freely, rather than brushing it out like a conventional oil paint.

Low-odour, solvent-based finishes have largely eradicated the smell and fumes associated with drying paint.

Fast-drying acrylic paints

Acrylic paints have several advantages over oil paints. Being water-based, they are non-flammable, practically odourless, and constitute less of a risk to health and the environment. They also dry very quickly.

Provided they are applied to adequately prepared wood or keyed paintwork, acrylic paints form a tough yet flexible coating. However, acrylic paints may not dry satisfactorily if they are applied on a damp or humid day. Even under perfect conditions, don't expect to achieve a high-gloss finish when using acrylic paints.

APPLYING THE PAINT

Prepare and prime all new woodwork thoroughly before applying the finishing coats. Wash down old paintwork with a sugar-soap solution and key gloss paint with wet-and-dry paper.

If you are using conventional oil paint, apply one or two undercoats, depending on the covering power of the paint. As each coat hardens, rub down with fine wet-and-dry paper to remove blemishes, then wipe the surface with a cloth dampened with white spirit.

Apply the paint with vertical strokes, then spread it sideways to even out the coverage. Finish with light strokes ('laying off') in the direction of the grain.

Blend the edges of the next application while the paint is still wet. Don't go back over a painted surface that has already started to dry, or you will leave brush marks in the paintwork.

Use a different technique for spreading one-coat or acrylic paints: simply lay on the paint liberally with almost parallel strokes, then lay off lightly. Blend wet edges quickly.

PAINTING THE DOOR

Doors have a variety of faces, edges and mouldings that need to be painted separately, yet the end result must look even in colour, with no ugly brush marks or heavily painted edges. Recommended procedures for painting different types of door will help you achieve those ends.

Getting ready

Remove the door handles and wedge the door open so that it cannot be closed accidentally, locking you in the room. Keep the handle in the room with you, just in case. Aim to paint the door and its frame separately, so that there is less chance of touching wet paintwork when passing through the freshly painted doorway. Paint the door first, then when it is dry finish the framework.

If you want to use a different colour for each side of the door, paint the hinged edge the colour of the closing face (the one that comes to rest against the frame). Paint the outer edge of the door the same colour as the opening face. This means that there won't be any difference in colour when the door is viewed from either side.

Avoiding runs

When painting up to the edge of a door or window frame, brush from the centre out: if you flex the bristles against the edge, the paint will run. Brushing across mouldings tends to flex the bristles unevenly and too much paint flows: spread the paint well, taking special care at the corners of moulded panels.

Painting a flush door

To paint a flush door, start at the top and work down in sections, blending each one into the other. Lay on the paint, then finish each section with light vertical brush strokes. Finally, paint the edges.

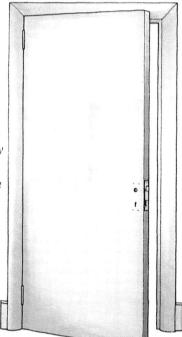

Painting a panelled door

Whatever the style of panelled door you are painting, start with the mouldings (1) followed by the panels (2). Paint the muntins (3) next, then the cross rails (4). Finish the face by painting the stiles (5). Finally, paint the edge of the door (6).

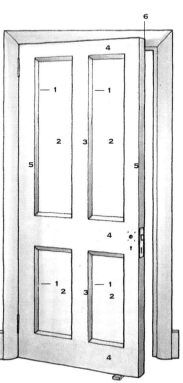

PAINTING A DOOR SURROUND

Each side of the frame should match the corresponding face of the door. Paint the frame in the room into which the door swings, including the edge of the stop bead against which the door closes, to match the opening face. Paint the rest of the frame the colour of the closing face.

Opening side
Paint the architrave (1) and doorframe up to and including the edge of the door stop (2) one colour. Paint the face of the door and its opening edge (3) the same colour.

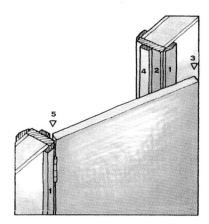

Opposite side
Paint the architrave and frame up to and over the door stop (4) the second colour. Paint the opposite face of the door and its hinged edge (5) with the second colour.

Glazed doors
Paint the glazing bars first, then the cross rails, and finish by painting the vertical stiles.

PAINTING UP TO GLASS

When painting the edge of glazing bars, it is usual to overlap the glass by about 2mm (1/16in) to prevent rain or condensation seeping between the glass and woodwork. However, if you find you can't make a neat job of it, try one of the following tips.

To achieve a satisfactory straight edge, use a proprietary plastic or metal paint shield, holding it against the edge of the frame to protect the glass.

Alternatively, run masking tape around the edges of the pane, leaving a slight gap so that the paint will seal the join between glass and frame. When the paint is touch-dry, carefully peel off the tape. Don't wait until the paint is completely dry, or it may peel off with the tape.

Once it has set, use a sharp blade to scrape off any paint that has accidentally dripped onto the glass. Many DIY stores sell plastic handles to hold disposable knife blades for this purpose.

GLASS SCRAPER

THE BOLD USE OF COLOUR HAS UNIFIED THIS
INTERIOR SCHEME AND DEMONSTRATES
MANY OF THE PAINTED WOODWORK
SITUATIONS THE AVERAGE HOUSEHOLDER
WILL COME ACROSS – WOOD PANELLING,
DOORS AND WINDOW FRAMES, SKIRTING
BOARDS AND STAIRS.

PAINTING A CASEMENT WINDOW

A casement window is hung on hinges and opens like a door, so if you plan to paint each side a different colour, follow a similar procedure to that described for painting doors and frames. Window frames need to be painted in strict order, so that the various components will be evenly treated, and also so you can close them at night. You also need to take care not to splash window panes with paint or apply a crooked line around the glazing bars – the mark of poor workmanship. Clean the glass in your windows before decorating to avoid picking up particles of dust in the paint.

Removing the handle and stay
Remove the stay and window catch before you paint the casement. So that you can still operate the window without touching wet paint, drive a nail into the underside of the bottom rail to act as a makeshift handle.

Temporary stay
Make a temporary stay with a length of stiff wire wrapped round the nail – hook the other end and slot it into one of the screw holes in the frame.

Applying the paint
First paint the glazing bars (1), overlapping the glass on each side (see page 98). Carry on with the top and bottom horizontal rails (2) followed by the vertical stiles (3). Finish the casement by painting the edges (4), then paint the frame (5).

PAINTING A SASH WINDOW

Sash windows are more difficult to paint than casements, as the two panes slide vertically, overlapping each other.

The following sequence describes the painting of a sash window from the inside. To paint the outside face, use a similar procedure but start with the lower sash. If you are using different colours for each side, the demarcation lines are fairly obvious: when the window is shut, all the visible surfaces from one side should be the same.

CUTTING-IN BRUSH

Following a logical sequence

Raise the bottom sash and pull down the top one. Paint the bottom meeting rail of the top sash (1) and the accessible parts of the vertical members (2). Reverse the position of the sashes, leaving a gap top and bottom, and complete the painting of the top sash (3). Paint the bottom sash (4), then the frame (5) except for the runners in which the sashes slide.

Leave the paint to dry, then paint the inner runners (6) plus a short section of the outer runners (7), pulling the cords aside to avoid splashing paint on them, as this makes them brittle. Before the paint dries, check that the window can slide.

RAISE THE BOTTOM SASH AND PULL DOWN THE TOP ONE

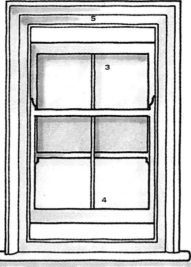

REVERSE THE POSITION OF THE SLIDING SASHES

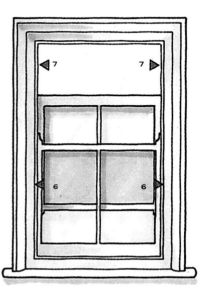

LOWER BOTH SASHES IN ORDER TO PAINT THE RUNNERS

REFURBISHING YOUR KITCHEN CABINETS

Essential tools
Paintbrush

A cheap and easy way to spruce up an old wood kitchen is to revarnish all the doors and drawer fronts. You can even change the appearance of the cabinets by applying a wood-coloured varnish.

THESE EXAMPLES DEMONSTRATE HOW DIFFERENT VARNISHES AFFECT THE SAME SPECIES OF WOOD.

Varnishing serves two main purposes: to protect wood from knocks, stains and other marks, and to give it a sheen that accentuates the beautiful grain pattern. As such, it is the ideal finish for fitted furniture that has to put up with a lot of wear and tear but which must also retain its good looks with the minimum of maintenance.

Colour samples
(above)
From left to right
Untreated softwood
Clear matt varnish
Clear gloss varnish
Wood-colour varnish
Tinted satin varnish
Pure-colour varnish

CHOOSING YOUR VARNISH

BRUSHING ON THE VARNISH

Modern varnishes are waterproof, scratchproof and heat-resistant, and are available in gloss, satin or matt finishes. Conventional varnishes are thinned with white spirit, but there are also fast-drying, water-thinned, acrylic varnishes that have an opaque, milky appearance when applied, but are clear and transparent when dry.

Some varnishes are designed to provide a clear finish with a hint of colour. They are available in the normal wood shades and some strong colours. Unlike a wood dye, a coloured varnish does not sink into the timber, so there may be loss of colour in areas of heavy wear or abrasion unless you apply an additional coat of clear varnish.

When dust sticks to the varnish
Sometimes it is difficult to prevent dust particles sticking to the varnish as it sets. Let the varnish set hard, then rub it down with very fine wire wool or abrasive paper. Apply a fresh coat of varnish to restore the finish – a second coat of coloured varnish may darken the wood. Use a similar procedure to correct any unsightly runs that show after the varnish has set.

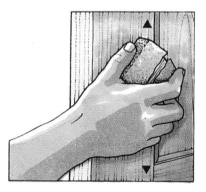

1 Lightly sand the old finish with fine wet-and-dry paper, taking care not to wear through to bare wood on the corners and edges. Make sure all surfaces are clean and grease-free.

Load a clean paintbrush by dipping the first third of the bristles into the varnish, then touch off the excess on the side of the container. Don't scrape the brush across the rim of the container as that causes bubbles in the varnish, which can spoil the finish if transferred to the woodwork.

2 Paint the varnish onto the work, brushing it in different directions to spread it evenly, then finish off by brushing lightly in the direction of the grain. Blend one section into the other before the varnish begins to set.

Essential tools

Craft knife

Paperhanger's brush

Paperhanger's scissors

Paste brush

Pasting table

Plumb line

Seam roller

Smoothing roller

Tape measure

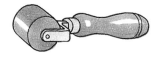

See also
Painting the ceiling, page 56
Papering the ceiling, page 54
Patching up
damaged plaster, page 74
Stripping old wallpaper, page 44

PAPERING THE SPARE ROOM

Although most people have few qualms about picking up a paintbrush, wallpapering seems to be far more daunting – a strange reaction when you consider that so much effort has gone into making things easy for us. All but hand-printed papers are ready trimmed to width, they are colour-fast, they won't stretch or tear provided you exercise a little care, and ready-mixed or liquid pastes remove all that worry about lumpy mixes.

Described here are the skills you need for papering a small bedroom with at least one window, a fireplace and one door, but once you have mastered these basic techniques you can wallpaper a room of any size.

A weekend should give you plenty of time – an experienced decorator can usually finish papering a small room in a day – assuming you have already stripped and filled the plasterwork, and either washed down the old paintwork or applied fresh paint the weekend before. Similarly, you will have either painted the ceiling with emulsion or already have hung new ceiling paper.

THE PRETTY PAPERED BEDROOM
MAKES USE OF CO-ORDINATED WALLPAPER
AND FABRICS. THE DECORATIVE BORDER,
AT DADO HEIGHT, CLEVERLY UNITES THE
WALLPAPER AND CURTAIN MOTIFS.

WHERE TO START

You may find it easiest to paper the longest uninterrupted wall to get used to the basic techniques before tackling corners or obstructions. Hang the first length of paper near one corner, and work away from the prevailing light.

Working with bold patterns
If your wallcovering has a large regular motif, centre the first length over the fireplace for symmetry. Alternatively, centre this first length between two windows, unless you will be left with narrow strips each side, in which case it's best to butt two lengths on the centre line.

CHOOSING THE RIGHT PASTE

Most wallpaper pastes are supplied in liquid form, or as powder or flakes for mixing with water.

All-purpose paste
Standard wallpaper paste is suitable for most lightweight to medium-weight papers. If you add less water, you can use it for hanging heavyweight papers.

Heavy-duty paste
This is specially prepared for hanging embossed papers, paper-backed fabrics and other heavyweight wallcoverings.

Fungicidal paste
Most pastes contain a fungicide to prevent mould growth under impervious wallcoverings such as vinyls, washable papers and foamed-plastic coverings.

Ready-mixed paste
Tubs of ready-mixed thixotropic paste are specially made for hanging heavyweight wallcoverings.

Liquid paste
Use a liquid wallpaper paste to avoid any possibility of a lumpy mix.

Repair adhesive
This paste is sold in tubes for sticking down peeling edges and corners. It even glues vinyl to vinyl.

Ready-pasted wallcoverings
Many wallcoverings come precoated with adhesive that is activated by soaking a cut length in a trough of cold water. Mix some ordinary paste to recoat dry edges.

PASTING THE PAPER

You can use any wipe-clean table for pasting, but a narrow fold-up pasting table is a good investment if you are going to do a lot of decorating.

1 Lay several cut lengths of paper face down on the table, to keep it clean. Tuck the ends under a length of string tied loosely round the table legs to stop the paper rolling up while you are pasting. Use a large, soft wall brush or pasting brush to apply the paste. Mix the paste in a plastic bucket and tie string across the rim to support the brush, keeping its handle clean while you hang the paper.

2 Align the wallpaper with the far edge of the table, so there will be no paste on the table to be transferred to the face of the paper. Apply the paste by brushing away from the centre, pasting the edges carefully and removing any lumps. If you prefer, apply the paste with a short-pile paint roller, pouring the paste into a roller tray and rolling in one direction only towards the end of the paper.

3 Pull the wallcovering to the front edge of the table and paste the other half. Fold the pasted end over – don't press it down – and slide the length along the table in order to expose the next unpasted part.

4 Paste the other end, then fold it over to almost meet the first cut end. The second fold is invariably deeper than the first – a good way to denote the bottom of patterned wallcoverings. Fold long drops concertina-fashion.

FOLD LONG PIECES CONCERTINA-FASHION

TIP • • • • • • • • • •
Leave the paper to soak Drape pasted paper over a broom handle spanning two chair backs, and leave them to soak. Some heavy coverings may need to soak for about 15 minutes. Hang vinyls and lightweight papers immediately.

THIS BOLDLY PATTERNED WALLPAPER HAS BEEN
CENTRED BETWEEN TWO WINDOWS (SEE PAGE 106).
A MATCHING DECORATIVE FRIEZE COVERS THE CUT
EDGE OF THE PAPER WHERE IT MEETS THE CEILING.

TRIMMING AND CUTTING

Most wallcoverings are machine-trimmed to width so that you can butt adjacent lengths accurately. Some hand-printed papers are left untrimmed. These are usually expensive, so it's not worth attempting to trim them yourself: ask the wallpaper supplier to do it for you.

Cutting plain wallpaper to length
Measure the height of the wall at the point where you will hang the first 'drop'. Add an extra 100mm (4in) for trimming top and bottom. Cut several pieces from your first roll to the same length and mark the top of each one.

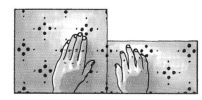

Allowing for patterned wallpaper
You may have to allow extra on alternate lengths of patterned wallpaper, in order to match the pattern.

STARTING WITH A STRAIGHT WALL

The walls of most rooms are rarely truly square, so use a plumb line to mark a vertical guide against which to hang the first length of wallcovering.

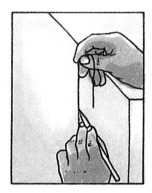

1 *Start at one end of the wall and mark the vertical line one roll width away from the corner, minus 12mm (½in) so the first length will overlap the adjacent wall.*

2 *Allowing enough wallcovering for trimming at the ceiling, unfold the top section of the pasted length and hold it against the plumbed line. Brush the paper gently onto the wall, working out from the centre in all directions to squeeze out any trapped air.*

3 *When you are sure the paper is positioned accurately, lightly draw the point of your scissors along the ceiling line, peel back the top edge and cut along the crease. Smooth the paper back, and stipple it down with the brush.*

4 *Unpeel the lower fold of the paper, smooth it onto the wall with the brush, then stipple it into the corner. Crease the bottom edge against the skirting, peel away the paper, then trim and brush it back against the wall.*

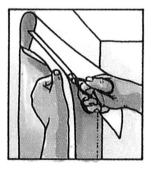

Hang the next length in the same manner. Slide it with your fingertips to align the pattern and produce a perfect butt joint. Wipe any paste from the surface with a damp cloth. Ensure that the edges of the paper adhere firmly by running a seam roller along the butt joint. Continue to the other end of the wall, allowing the last drop to overlap the adjoining wall by 12mm (½in).

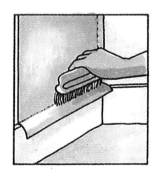

HOME-MADE PLUMB LINE

PAPERING AROUND THE CORNER

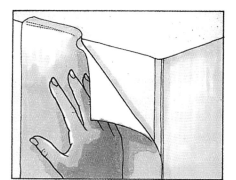

1 Turn the corner by marking another plumbed line, so that the next length of paper covers the overlap from the first wall. If the piece you trimmed off at the corner is wide enough, use it as your first length on the new wall.

2 If there's an alcove on both sides of the fireplace, you will need to wrap the paper around the external corners. Trim the last length so that it wraps around the corner, lapping the next wall by about 25mm (1in). Plumb and hang the remaining strip with its edge about 12mm (½in) from the corner.

PAPERING AROUND RADIATORS, SWITCHES AND SOCKETS

There are always small details to contend with as you paper the main areas of the room.

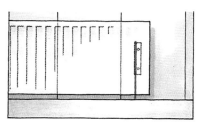

Papering behind the radiator
If you cannot remove a radiator, turn off the heating and allow it to cool. Use a steel tape to measure the positions of the brackets fixing the radiator to the wall. Transfer these measurements to a length of wallcovering and slit it from the bottom to the top of the bracket. Feed the pasted paper behind the radiator, down both sides of the brackets. Use a radiator roller to press it to the wall. Crease and trim to the skirting board.

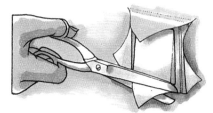

Papering around switches and sockets
To be safe, turn off the electricity at the mains. Hang the wallcovering over the switch or socket. Make diagonal cuts from the centre of the fitting to each of its corners and tap the excess paper against the edges of the faceplate with the brush. Trim off the waste, leaving 6mm (¼in) all round. Loosen the faceplate, tuck the margin behind and retighten it.

PAPERING AROUND THE DOOR AND WINDOWS

When you get to the door, hang the length of paper beside the doorframe, brushing down the butt joint to align the pattern and allowing the other edge to loosely overlap the door.

1   Make a diagonal cut in the excess towards the top corner of the frame. Crease the waste down the side of the frame with scissors, peel it back, trim off and then brush back. Leave a 12mm (½in) strip for turning on the top of the frame.

2   Fill in with short strips above the door, then butt the next full length of paper over the door and cut the excess diagonally into the frame, pasting the rest of this strip down the side of the door. Mark and cut off the waste.

  Treat a flush window frame the same way as the door. But if the window is set into a reveal, hang the length of wallcovering next to the window and allow it to overhang the opening. Make a horizontal cut just above the edge of the window reveal. Make a similar cut near the bottom, then fold the paper around to cover the side of the reveal. Crease and trim along the window frame and sill.

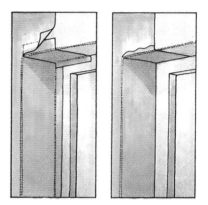

1   To fill in the window reveal, first cut a strip of paper to match the width and pattern of the overhang just above the reveal. Paste the strip, slip it under the overhang and fold it around the top of the reveal.

2   Cut through the overlap with a smooth, wavy stroke, then remove the excess paper and roll down the joint. To continue, hang short lengths on the wall below and above the window, wrapping top lengths into the reveal.

TIMESAVER TIP • • • • • • • • • • • •

Papering around the fireplace
Papering around a fireplace is similar to fitting the paper around a door. Make a diagonal cut in the waste overlapping the fireplace, cutting towards the corner of the mantel shelf. Now tuck the paper in all round for creasing and trimming to the fireplace surround.

  If the surround is fairly ornate, first brush the paper onto the wall above the surround, then trim the paper to fit under the mantel shelf at each side; brush the paper around the corners of the chimney breast to hold it in place. Now gently press the wallpaper into the shape of the fire surround, then peel it away and cut round the impression with nail scissors. Smooth the paper back down with the brush.

HANGING VINYL WALLPAPER

Paste paper-backed vinyls in the normal way. Cotton-backed vinyl hangs better if you paste the wall and then leave it to become tacky before you apply the wallcovering. Use fungicidal paste.

Hang and butt-join lengths of vinyl, using a sponge, rather than a brush, to smooth them onto the wall. Crease a length top and bottom, then trim it to size with a sharp knife.

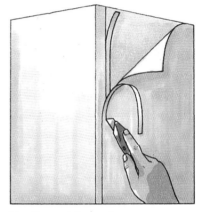

Dealing with overlaps
Vinyl will not normally stick to itself, so when you turn a corner use a knife to cut through both pieces of paper where they overlap. Peel away the excess and rub down the vinyl to produce a perfect butt joint.

Vinyls and other wallcoverings
Below (anticlockwise):
Washable papers
Vinyl wallcoverings
Paper-backed fabrics

Cork-faced paper
Grass-cloth effects
Flock papers
Foamed polyethylene

VINYL WALLCOVERINGS ARE THE IDEAL SOLUTION FOR
BATHROOMS WHERE A WATER RESISTANT, STEAMPROOF
AND EASY WIPEDOWN SURFACE IS REQUIRED.

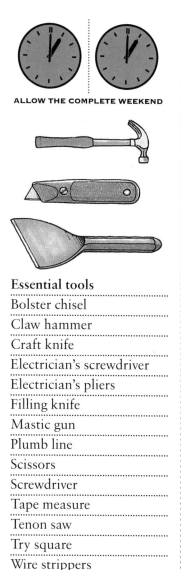

Essential tools

Bolster chisel

Claw hammer

Craft knife

Electrician's screwdriver

Electrician's pliers

Filling knife

Mastic gun

Plumb line

Scissors

Screwdriver

Tape measure

Tenon saw

Try square

Wire strippers

BLOCKING OUT NOISY NEIGHBOURS

Noise generated by thoughtless neighbours can make life distinctly unpleasant, if not intolerable. Although it is difficult to block out unwelcome sounds completely, it is possible to reduce the amount of noise passing through a shared wall.

Sealing gaps

Sealing gaps in the shared or party wall is one obvious way to reduce airborne noise. If necessary, remove skirtings and floorboards close to the party wall so you can repoint poor mortar joints and fill any gaps around joists that are built into the masonry. After replacing the skirting and floorboards, seal any gaps between them with a flexible mastic.

It may also be worth repointing the wall in the loft, and plastering it to add mass.

Detached insulated lining
1 Head plate
2 Sole plate
3 Studs
4 Insulating blanket
5 Nogging
6 First layer of plasterboard
7 Second layer of plasterboard
8 Electrical fitting

LINING THE WALL

The soundproofing of a party wall can be greatly improved by building an insulated lining. However, its effectiveness will depend to some extent on the construction of the wall, whether or not there is a fireplace, the location of electrical or plumbing fittings, and the proximity of windows.

The lining – constructed in a similar way to an ordinary stud partition – is fixed to the floor, ceiling and side walls, but not to the party wall itself. The gap between the lining and the wall is filled with glass-fibre or mineral-fibre blanket insulation, and the lining is clad with two layers of plasterboard.

Adding a lining to the party wall of an older house may mean having to modify a moulded-plaster cornice; and the size of the room will be reduced, whatever the age of the house. Nevertheless, the benefits are likely to compensate for the disadvantages and effort involved.

What to do first

Switch off the electrical supply at the consumer unit, and replace any fittings attached to the party wall with junction boxes in readiness for relocating the fittings on the new lining. If your experience is limited, hire an electrician to do the electrical work for you.

Remove the skirting carefully for reuse. Mark a line on the ceiling 100mm (4in) from the party wall. Drop a plumb line and make a similar mark on the floor below.

Fixing the lining sole plate to the floor presents few problems; but if the ceiling joists run parallel to the party wall, then you may have to nail noggings (stout battens) between them to provide secure fixing points for the lining head plate.

Erecting the lining

Nail a 75 x 50mm (3 x 2in) softwood head plate and sole plate in position, with their front edges on the marked lines – this will leave a 25mm (1in) gap between them and the wall. Nail matching vertical studs between them at 600mm (2ft) intervals. Mark the position of each stud on the floor and ceiling to help you relocate them when fixing the plasterboard.

Hang floor-to-ceiling lengths of 100 x 600mm (4in x 2ft) insulating blanket between the studs, tucking the edges behind the framework. Skew-nail noggings between the studs to serve as fixing points for shelving or electrical mounting boxes.

Check that the power is still switched off at the consumer unit, then run short lengths of cable from junction boxes to the new mounting-box locations.

Cover the framework with plasterboard 12mm (½in) thick. Fill the joints and seal around the outer edges with mastic. Nail a second layer of tapered-edge boards over the first, staggering the joints and placing the nails about 150mm (6in) apart.

Fill and tape the joints between the boards, then nail the skirting board in place. Mount and wire the electrical fittings, sealing around the edges of flush-mounted electrical mounting boxes with mastic. Seal the lower edge of the skirting board, too.

TILING THE BATHROOM

Waterproof ceramic tiles are an obvious choice for lining showers or for other areas of a bathroom that will be splashed with water, and there's an almost inexhaustible range of colours, textures and patterns to choose from.

The majority of tiles are square, the dimensions varying according to use and the manufacturer's preference. Rectangular and more irregularly shaped tiles are also available, and coving tiles are sometimes used to cover the joint between the wall and a bath or basin, or for finishing the edge of a half-tiled wall.

It takes very little time to hang even a fairly large area of tiles, but the work becomes far more time-consuming when you have to cut and fit border tiles and accommodate bathroom fittings and accessories.

TILE SAW

Essential tools

Home-made gauge stick

Adhesive spreader

Tile cutter

Tile saw

Grout spreader

Tile nibblers

Tile-cutting jig

Claw hammer

Spirit level

Plumb line

TILE CUTTER

FIELD TILE FOR GENERAL TILING WITH SPACING LUGS MOULDED ONTO IT

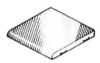

ROUNDED-EDGE (RE) TILE FOR EDGING THE FIELD

REX TILE WITH TWO ADJACENT ROUNDED EDGES

UNIVERSAL TILE WITH TWO GLAZED, SQUARE EDGES FOR USE IN ANY POSITION

QUADRANT TILE TO FILL THE JOINT BETWEEN BATH AND WALL

MITRED TILE USED AT THE END IF YOU WANT TO TURN A CORNER

BULLNOSE TILE FOR FINISHING THE END OF A STRAIGHT RUN

See also:
Patching up
damaged plaster, page 74
Stripping old wallpaper, page 44

GETTING PREPARED

The walls of your bathroom must be clean, sound and dry. You cannot tile over wallpaper, and you need to coat flaking or powdery paint with a stabilizing primer to make a suitable base for the tiles. It is important that you make the surface as flat as possible, so the tiles will stick firmly. Setting out the prepared surface accurately is vital to hanging the tiles properly.

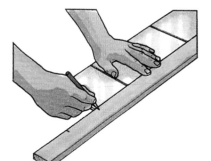

Making a gauge stick
First make a gauge stick (a tool for plotting the position of tiles on the wall) from a length of 50 x 12mm (2 x ½in) softwood. Lay several tiles beside it – butting together those with lugs, or adding spacers if the tiles are square-edged – and mark the position of each tile along the softwood batten.

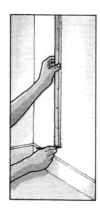

Using the gauge stick
Holding the gauge stick firmly against the wall, mark the positions of the tiles on the surface.

SETTING OUT THE WALL TILES

The way you set out the walls of your bathroom depends on the scale and shape of the area you are tiling. To tile a plain uninterrupted wall, for example, use the gauge stick to plan horizontal rows starting at skirting level. If you are left with a narrow strip at the top, move the rows up half a tile width to create a wider margin.

1 *Mark the bottom of the lowest row of whole tiles. Temporarily nail a thin guide batten to the wall, aligned with the mark. Make sure it is horizontal by placing a spirit level on top.*

2 *Mark the centre of the wall, then use the gauge stick to set out the rows of tiles on each side of it. If the border tiles measure less than half a width, reposition the rows sideways by half a tile.*

3 *Use a spirit level to position a guide batten against the last vertical line, and nail it to the wall.*

4 *If you are tiling part of a wall only (up to a dado rail, for example), start by setting out a row of whole tiles at the top. This is particularly important if you plan to use RE tiles.*

5 *If you have to accommodate a window in your scheme, use it as your starting point so that the tiles surrounding it are equal in size – but not too narrow. If possible, begin a row of whole tiles at sill level.*

6 *Position cut tiles at the back of the window reveal.*

7 *Fix a guide batten over a window to position a row of tiles temporarily.*

TIP ● ● ● ● ● ● ● ● ● ● ● ● ● ● ● ● ● ●
Avoid cutting difficult shapes
Check with the gauge stick how the tiles will fit round pipes and other obstructions. Make slight adjustments to the position of the main field to avoid difficult shaping around these features.

Setting out walls for tiling
It is possible to plan different arrangements of wall tiles, using a home-made gauge stick. Try to ensure a wide margin all round.

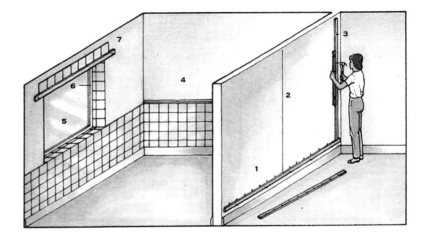

TILING
THE WALLS

Most ceramic-tile adhesives are sold ready-mixed, although a few need to be mixed with water. The tubs or packets will state the coverage.

Use a waterproof tile adhesive in a bathroom or shower. Some adhesives can also be used for grouting (filling the joints between the tiles). A notched adhesive spreader is usually supplied with each tub, or you can use a special serrated trowel.

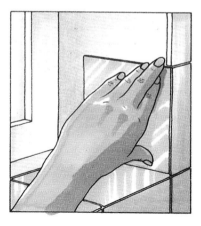

Tiling around a window
Tile up to the edges of a window, then stick RE tiles to the reveal so that they lap the edges of surrounding tiles. Fill in any space left between the edging tiles and the window with cut tiles.

SERRATED TROWEL

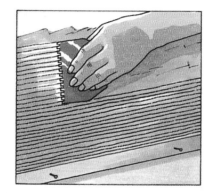

1 Spread enough adhesive on the wall to cover about 1 metre (3ft) square. Press the toothed edge of the spreader against the wall surface and drag it through the adhesive so that it forms horizontal ridges.

2 Press the first tile into the angle formed by the setting-out battens until it is firmly fixed, then butt up tiles on each side. Build up three or four rows at a time. If the tiles do not have lugs, place proprietary plastic spacers between them to provide space for grouting.

Wipe away adhesive from the surface of the tiles with a damp sponge. Spread more adhesive, and tile along the batten until the first rows of whole tiles are complete. From time to time, check that your tiling is accurate by holding a batten and spirit level across the faces and along the top and side edges.

When you have completed the main area, scrape adhesive from the borders and allow the rest to set before removing the setting-out battens and proceeding with marking out and cutting border tiles.

CUTTING BORDER TILES

Having finished the main field of tiles, it is necessary to cut border tiles one at a time to fit the gaps between the field tiles and the adjacent walls (since walls are hardly ever truly square, the margin is bound to be uneven). Protect your eyes with safety spectacles or goggles when snapping scored ceramic tiles.

1 Mark a border tile by placing it face down over its neighbour, with one edge against the adjacent wall. Make an allowance for normal spacing between the tiles. Transfer the marks to the edge of the tiles using a felt-tip pen.

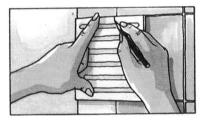

2 Use a proprietary tile cutter, held against a straightedge, to score across the face with one firm stroke to cut through the glaze. You may also have to score the edges of thick tiles.

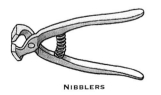

NIBBLERS

3 Stretch a length of thin wire across a panel of chipboard, place the scored line directly over the wire and press down on both sides to snap the tile. Smooth the cut edges of the tile with a tile sander or small slipstone.

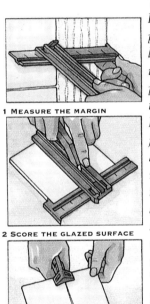

1 MEASURE THE MARGIN

2 SCORE THE GLAZED SURFACE

3 SNAP THE TILE

Tile-cutting jig
If you are planning to do a lot of tiling, it is worth buying a purpose-made tile-cutting jig. Inexpensive plastic jigs are perfectly adequate for relatively thin tiles, but you can also buy more substantial jigs that will cut tiles of any thickness. These jigs enable you to score tiles accurately and snap them with ease every time.

Cutting thin strips
A cutting jig is the most accurate tool for cutting a thin strip cleanly from the edge of a tile. If you do not want to use the strip itself, chip away the waste a little at a time with tile nibblers.

CUTTING TILES TO FIT AROUND APPLIANCES

Cutting border tiles is relatively easy, but you will have to perfect different techniques to fit wall tiles around pipes and appliances.

Fitting around a pipe

Try to set out tiles so that you can cut semi-circles from the edges of two adjacent tiles.

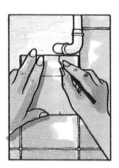

2 Make one straight cut through the centre of the circle and either nibble out the waste, having scored the curve, or clamp it in a vice, protected with softening, and cut it out with a tile saw. Stick one half of the tile on each side of the pipe.

1 If that is not possible, mark the centre of the pipe on the top and side edges of a tile and draw lines across the tile from these points. Where they cross, draw round a coin or something slightly larger than the diameter of the pipe.

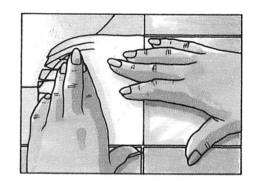

Cutting a curve

To fit a tile against a curved shape, cut a template from thin card to the exact size of a tile. Cut 'fingers' along one edge; press them against the curve to reproduce the shape. Transfer the curve onto the face of the tile and cut away the waste with a tile saw (instead of a blade, this has a thin metal rod, coated with hard abrasive particles, that will cut in any direction).

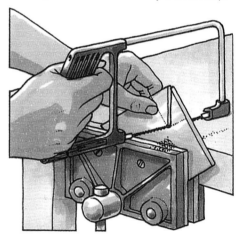

Fitting around a shaver socket

You may have to cut a square or oblong piece from one corner of a tile in order to fit around a shaver socket. Mark it from the socket, then clamp the tile in a vice, protected with softening. Score both lines, then use a saw file to make one diagonal cut from the corner of the tile to where the lines meet. Snap out both triangles.

If you have to cut a notch out of a large tile, cut down both sides with a hacksaw, then score between them and snap the piece out of the middle.

GROUTING THE TILES AND SEALING THE GAPS

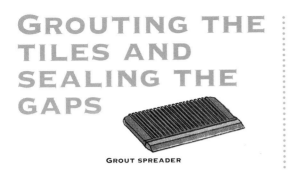

GROUT SPREADER

Use a ready-mixed paste called grout to fill the gaps between the tiles. Standard grouts are white, grey or brown, but there is also a limited range of coloured grouts to match or contrast with the tiles. If you need to match a particular colour, mix pigments into a dry powdered grout, and then add water. Waterproof grout is essential for showers and bath surrounds.

Spreading the grout
Leave the tile adhesive to harden for 24 hours, then use a rubber-bladed spreader to press grout into the joints. Spread it in all directions to make sure all the joints are well filled.

Wipe grout from the surface of the tiles with a sponge before it sets. Smooth the joints with a blunt-ended stick – use a knife and abrasive paper to shape one end of a dowel. When the grout has dried, polish the tiles with a dry cloth.

Leave the grout to harden for about a week before using a tiled shower.

SEALING AROUND BATHROOM FITTINGS

It's best not to use grout to seal the gap between a tiled wall and shower tray, bath or basin – the fittings can flex sufficiently to crack a rigid seal, and allow water to seep in. Instead, use a silicone-rubber caulking compound to fill the gaps. The compound, which is packed in cartridges with pointed nozzles, remains flexible enough to accommodate any movement. These sealants are available in a choice of colours to match tiles and bathroom fittings, and can cope with gaps up to 3mm (⅛in) wide.

Using a sealant
Trim the end off the plastic nozzle (the amount you cut off dictates the thickness of the bead) and press the tip into the joint at an angle of 45 degrees. Push forward at a steady rate while squeezing the applicator's trigger or the base of the cartridge itself to apply a bead of sealant. Smooth any ripples with the handle of a wetted teaspoon.

GLOSSARY OF TERMS

Airlock
A blockage in a pipe caused by a trapped bubble of air.

Architrave
The moulding around a door or window.

Batt
A short cut length of glass-fibre or mineral-fibre insulation.

Cavity wall
A wall of two separate masonry 'skins' with an air space between them.

Countersink
To cut a tapered recess that allows the head of a woodscrew to lie flush with a surface; or, the tapered recess itself.

Damp-proof course – DPC
A layer of impervious material which prevents moisture rising from the ground into the walls of a building.

Damp-proof membrane – DPM
A layer of impervious material which prevents moisture rising through a concrete floor.

Datum point
The point from which measurements are taken.

Drop
A strip of paper cut ready for pasting to a wall.

Fall
A downward slope.

Hardcore
Broken bricks or stones used to form a sub-base below paving.

Lath and plaster
A method of finishing a timber-framed wall or ceiling. Narrow strips of wood are nailed to the studs or joists to provide a supporting framework for the plaster.

Mastic
A nonsetting compound used to seal joints.

Mullion
A vertical dividing member of a window frame.

Muntin
A central vertical member of a panel door.

Nogging
A short horizontal wooden member between studs.

Nosing
The front edge of a stair tread.

Party wall
The wall between two houses over which each of the adjoining owners has equal rights.

Primer
The first coat of a paint system which protects the workpiece and reduces absorption of subsequent applications.

Reveal
The vertical side of an opening in a wall.

Riser
The vertical part of a step.

Sash
The openable part of a window.

Stile
A vertical side member of a door or window sash.

Stud partition
An interior timber-framed dividing wall.

Thixotropic paints
Non-drip paints that have a jelly-like consistency until stirred or applied – at which point they liquefy.

Trap
A bent section of pipe situated below a bath, washbasin or sink. A trap contains standing water that prevents the passage of gases.

Tread
The horizontal part of a step.

Undercoat
A layer of paint used to obliterate the colour of a primer and to build a protective body of paint prior to the application of a top coat.

A

abrasives 12, 45, 47, 59, 75, 103
acetone 12
acrylic lacquer 12
adhesives 59–60, 79, 120, 123
adhesive tape 20, 39, 41, 81
airing cupboard 19, 21
alcoves 71, 73, 110
aluminium spirit-based sealer 45, 57
aluminium weather trim 63
ammonia 12

B

bank of shelving 72–73
bathroom 21, 40–42, 117–123
battens 70–71, 119
beeswax polish 46
black lead 25
blade seal 67
blanket insulation 78–79
blanking plug 23
bleach solution 44
bleed valve 23
blinds 31–33
blockages 14–16
blockboard 69–70
blocked sink 14
blocked radiator valve 23
boiler 21, 23
bolts 35, 47, 51, 53
brackets 30, 32, 33, 70–73
brass fittings 10–12
British Standard 19, 34
brush seal 63, 65, 67
burglars 50–53
butyl sealant 75
Bylaw 30 kit 80

C

carnauba wax 46
carpet-fitting 38–39, 60
cast-iron door knocker 10, 13
cast-iron grate 25
cavity fixings 30, 72
ceilings 30, 54–57, 78, 94, 104
cellulose fibre insulation 80
central-heating expansion tank 80
chemical drain cleaner 14
chemical paint remover 13, 47
chipboard 69, 78
cisterns 17, 36–37, 42, 79–80
cleaning fluids 10
cold-water cisterns 79–80

concrete floor 39, 41, 63, 90–91
condensation 80, 98
cork granules 80
corners 106, 110
corrosion 11–13, 22–23, 25
cracks 74–75
curtain rails 28–30
cylinder jacket 80

D

damp-proof course 41, 86
Danish oil 47
datum pegs 87
deadbolts 34
deathwatch beetle 78
decorative details 25
decorator's trestle 54
detached insulated lining 114
detergent 11, 15, 45
diaphragm valve 18, 36–37
disinfectant 15
distemper 57
doors
    aluminium sliding 53
    back 34
    draughtproofing 62–65
    exterior 62, 63
    fittings 10–13
    flush 97
    frame 11, 64, 98
    front 10, 24, 34
    furniture 10
    glazed 53, 98
    handles 97
    interior 62, 64
    kits 63
    knockers 10, 13
    mouldings 41
    painting 10, 97–98
    panelled 97
    papering round 111
    pull 10
    right-handed opening 34
    sealing 64
    side 34
    stile 34
    surround 98
    ways 42
double glazing 81
double-sided adhesive tape 39, 41, 81
drain auger 16
drainage 86
draught excluder 63–64, 67, 79
draughtproofing sealant 64

draughtproofing 60, 62–65
draughts 28, 60, 62–65, 66–67, 78
dripping tap 21–22
dust sheets 56, 94

E

eaves 79–80
electrical fittings 45, 78–79, 80, 110, 115
energy saving 62, 66, 78, 81
escutcheons 35
exfoliated vermiculite 80
expanded-metal mesh 76
expanding-foam filler 67

F

fillers 74–75, 81
finishing oil 47
fireplace 25, 110–111, 115
flap valves 36–37
float 17–18, 36
float arm 17–18, 36–37
float valve 36–37
floorboards 38, 41, 58, 60, 114
flushing lever 36–37
foam strip insulation 64
foamed-plastic tubes 19–20, 38, 112
French polish 46
fungicidal paste 106, 112
furniture beetle 78

G

gaps, filling 62, 64, 67, 75, 79–80, 114, 121, 123
garden furniture 47
gauge stick 118–119
glass 69, 98
glass-fibre blanket 79–80, 115
goggles 13, 15, 121
graphite 25
grate polish 25
gravel 86
gripper strips 39
grooved metal angle 70
grooved metal T-section 70
grouting 120–123
guide batten 119
guide lines 54, 72, 86–87, 91

H

hairline cracks 75
hardcore 86

INDEX

headgear nut 21, 22
headrail 33
heat loss 62, 66, 78, 81horizontal blinds 33
hot-water cylinder 19, 21
hydraulic pump 16

I

immersion heater 21
inlet valve 23
insulation 19–20, 28, 78–80, 115

J

joints 47, 59–60, 86
joists 30, 77, 78, 80, 114

K

keyholes 35, 53, 65
kitchen flooring 40–42
kitchen cabinets 102–103
knee kicker 38

L

lacquers 10, 12
lagging 19–20, 80
landings 58
laths 76
"laying off" 96
letter boxes 65
letter plates 10, 12–13
light fittings 55, 79
lighter fluid 12
lippings 70, 73
liquid wax 46
living room, painting 92–101
locks 34–35, 50, 52–53, 65
loft 78–80
loose-fill insulation 78, 80
lugs 118, 120

M

mall slipstone 121
man-made boards 69, 71
marking gauge 35
masking tape 12, 98
masonry bit 72
mastic 79, 114–115
medium-density fibreboard (MDF) 69
metal extrusions 70
metal lintels 30
metal polish 11, 12
metallic inks 45

mica 80
mineral wool 80
mineral-fibre blanket
insulation 19, 79, 115
mobile platforms 57
mortar 87, 91
mould growth 44, 47, 106
mouldings 47, 60, 97

N

nail punch 60
natural stones 84, 90
noggings 30, 72, 115
noise 28, 112, 114–116
nosing 60

O

oil finish 47
one-piece siphon 37
outlet valve 23
overflow 17–18, 36

P

paint
  acrylic 92, 96
  brushes 57, 95
  emulsion 45, 57, 75, 92, 94–95, 104
    gloss 96, 103
    liquid 94, 96
    matt 13, 94, 103
    new-plaster emulsion 94
    oil 45, 96
    one-coat 92, 96
    satin 94, 96, 103
    solvent-based 92, 96
    stripping 13, 47
    rollers 95
    runs 97, 103
    shield 96, 98
    strippers 10
    textured 75
    thixotropic 94, 96
    tray 95
painted pressed steel 69
painting
  casement windows 100
  ceilings 56–57
  doors 10, 97
  door surround 98
  glass 98
  living room 92–101
  sash windows 101
  walls 92, 94
  woodwork 92
paper-backed fabrics 106, 112
papering 54–55, 104–113
partition wall 30, 75

patching 73, 74–77
paths 90–91
patios 84–90
paving slabs 84–88, 90
peephole viewer, fitting 24
pipes
  branch 15–16
  cold-water 20–21, 79–80
  flush 36–37
  hot-water 19–20
  insulation 19, 79–80
  lagging 20
  old water 80
  overflow 17–18
  profile gauge 41
  tiling round 119, 122
  waste 14–15
plaster 74–77, 78, 104, 114
plasterboard 76, 115
plumb line 72, 108, 110, 115
plunger 15
plywood 69–70, 80
polish 12, 25, 46
polyurethane foam 64
primer 13, 57, 92, 96, 117
profile gauge 41
protective gloves 10, 13, 15, 78
PVC 40, 64
PVC adhesive tape 20

Q

quadrant moulding 41

R

rack bolts 53
radiators 23, 110
repointing 114
revarnishing 102
risers, stairs 59–60
rock fibre 79
roller blinds 32
roof timbers 78
rot 78
rust – see corrosion
rust-inhibiting primer 13

S

safety spectacles 121
salt and vinegar solution 11
sand base 86, 91
scaffolding 54, 57
scoring 45
scraping 44–45, 75
screeding 41
screwed metal angle 70
screwed metal T-section 70
sealant 64, 75, 123

seam roller 109
secondary glazing systems 81
security 24, 34, 50–53
security chain, fitting 24
shaver socket 122
shelves 68–73, 115
silicone-rubber caulking
compound 123
sink overflow 16
siphon 36
skirting board 39, 41, 75, 96,
109–110, 114–115, 119
softening 122
sole plate 44–45
soundproofing 114–115
spacers 87, 118, 120
spare room, papering
104–113
spirit level 72–73, 91, 119–120
spring strip 64, 67
stairs 58–60
staples 52
stays 50, 52, 100
steam stripper 44–45
stepladder 54, 57, 94
stone pathway 90
stone paving 91
stopcock 21
straightedge 77, 87, 91, 121
stratified rock 90
string lines 86, 87, 91
stripping 13, 44–45, 47
stud partition 115
studs 72, 77, 115
sugar-soap solution 96

T

taps 21–22
taped film 81
tapered-edge boards 115
teak oil 47
textured glass 69
thixotropic paste 106
threshold bar 39, 41
tiles 115, 117–123
tinsnips 76
toilet cistern 17, 36–37, 42
traps 15–16
treads, stairs 59–60
tree resin 47
trimming 108, 110–111

U

undercoat 92, 96
underlay 38–40
uprights 71, 73

V

VA woodworking adhesive
60
varnish 46–47, 102–103
veneer 69–70
Venetian blinds 33
ventilation 51–52, 62, 79, 81
vents 79–80
verdigris 11
vertical blinds 33
vinyl 40–42, 45, 94, 106–107,
112

W

walkway boarding 80
walls
    brackets 72
    brush 107
    fixings 73
    lath-and-plaster 75
    masonry 30, 72
    painting 92, 94
    partition 30, 114–115
    party 115
    plasterboard 77
    plugs 30, 72
    soundproofing 114–115
    straight 108
    stud 76
    tiling 119–120
wallpaper
    backing 45
    cutting 108
    embossed 106
    flock 112
    hand-printed 108
    heavyweight 106
    lightweight 107
    lining 45, 56
    machine-trimmed 108
    painted 45
    paste 45, 104, 106
    pasted 55, 106
    pasting 107
    patterned 106, 108
    spare room 104
    stripping 44–45
    washable 45, 106, 112
washbasin 14–16, 42
washers 21, 22
washing soda 11
water-cylinder jacket 19
water-inlet valve 17
water-storage cistern 17
wax polish 46
weather bar 63
weathering 47
wet-and-dry paper 96, 103

white spirit 46, 96, 103
windows
    bay 30
    burglars 50–53
    casement 30, 51, 66, 100
    catch 100
    curtain rails 28
    draughty 66–67
    fanlight 52
    flush 111
    frames 97, 100
    French 53
    handles 100
    keys 50–51
    locks 51
    metal 50, 52
    painting 96, 101
    panes 100
    papering 106, 111
    pivot 67
    recess 32–33
    reveal 111
    runners 101
    sash 30, 50–51, 66–67, 81,
101
    sloping 33
    tiling round 119–120
    wooden 50, 52
wire link 36–37
wire wool 11, 13, 46–47 103
wired glass 69
wiring 79
wood 35, 41, 46–47, 60, 69,
70–71, 96, 102–103, 118
woodworm 78
work platform 54–57, 94

ACKNOWLEDGMENTS

The authors and editors
would like to thank the following for
their assistance in making this book:

STUDIO PHOTOGRAPHY
Paul Chave
Ben Jennings
Neil Waving
ARTWORK
Robin Harris
PAGE MAKEUP
Amanda Allchin
INDEX
AND PROOF READING
Mary Morton
PICTURE RESEARCH
Ella Jennings

Special thanks to the following companies
and individuals who contributed additional photographs
and product information to this book:

IDEAL STANDARD (BATHROOMS)
The Bathroom Works, National Avenue,
Kingston upon Hull,
pages 17, 31, 113.
FIRED EARTH (TILES AND INTERIORS)
Twyford Mill, Oxford Road, Adderbury, Oxfordshire.
pages 28, 77, 93, 99, 116, 117.
SUNWAY/LUXAFLEX (BLINDS)
Hunter Douglas (Window Fashions)
Mersey Industrial Estate, Heaton Mersey, Stockport, Cheshire, page 31.
NAIRN (CUSHION FLOORING)
Forbo-Nairn Limited, PO Box 1, Kircaldy, Scotland, page 43.
BARLOW TYRIE LIMITED (TEAKWOOD OUTDOOR FURNITURE)
Braintree, Essex, pages 47, 89.
LANGLOWS (WOOD FINISHES)
Products Division, Palace Chemicals Ltd.
Chesterton, Bucks, Page 58.
CUPRINOL LTD.(WOOD PRESERVATIVES)
Frome, Somerset, page 59.
© DAVID IRELAND, LANDSCAPE ARCHITECT,
David Mews, Greenwich South Street, London
Pages 85,89, 90.
© Colin Philp (Photographer), Page 85.
SANDERSON (WALLPAPERS)
6, Cavendish Square, London W1, Pages 105,108.
© Inklink (Ben Jennings Photography),
Jacket & pages 2, 4, 6, 7, 8, 9, 26, 27, 48, 49, 77, 82, 83, 118.